THE AUSTRALIAN
Women's Weekly

Low CARB
DINNERS

BAUER MEDIA GROUP

Published in 2017 by Bounty Books based on materials licensed to it by Bauer Media Books, Australia.

Bauer Media Books are published by
Bauer Media Pty Limited
54 Park St, Sydney; GPO Box 4088,
Sydney, NSW 2001 Australia
phone +61 2 9282 8618; fax +61 2 9126 3702
www.awwcookbooks.com.au

Publisher
Jo Runciman

Editorial & food director
Sophia Young

Director of sales, marketing & rights
Brian Cearnes

Editorial director-at-large
Pamela Clark

Creative director & designer
Hannah Blackmore

Managing editor
Stephanie Kistner

Junior editor
Amanda Lees

Food editor
Alexandra Elliott

Operations manager
David Scotto

Printed in China
by Leo Paper Products Ltd.

Published and distributed in the
United Kingdom by Bounty Books,
a division of Octopus Publishing Group Ltd
Carmelite House
50 Victoria Embankment
London, EC4Y 0DZ
United Kingdom
info@octopus-publishing.co.uk;
www.octopusbooks.co.uk

International foreign language rights
Brian Cearnes, Bauer Media Books
bcearnes@bauer-media.com.au

A catalogue record for this book is
available from the British Library.
ISBN: 978-0-75373-260-1

© Bauer Media Pty Ltd 2017
ABN 18 053 273 546

Low
CARB
DINNERS

Bounty
BOOKS

CONTENTS

LOW CARB FOR LIFE

How to eat healthily — either to simply maintain good health, or to lose weight in order to gain good health — is the holy grail of questions in the diet world, not only for people like you and I, but also for the medical fraternity at large. And the answer to this question is constantly evolving.

Up until quite recently a low-fat diet was considered the gold standard of the dieting world. The theory behind it was quite simple; gram for gram, fat has double the kilojoules of either protein or carbohydrates, therefore restricting fat meant one had more kilojoules available for either carbohydrates or protein. The problem with this diet was not the theory itself, but rather its execution. Since low-fat foods tend to be to bland-tasting, the food industry had to devise a way to add flavour back into their products. The solution: sugar, refined carbohydrates and a whole arsenal of other additives were included, which ended up having the reverse effect on our waist lines. Another real difficulty with low-fat diets is that they require tremendous amounts of willpower that few possess; they tend to leave us feeling hungry and more vulnerable to the very things that we might be trying to avoid. And so you can see how easily a cycle of yo-yo dieting might begin.

Enter the low-carbohydrate or low-carb diet. In order to understand the principle of the diet it is necessary to understand the function of carbohydrates in the body. Carbs, or carbohydrates, are macronutrients the body needs to function properly; the main micronutrients the body needs are carbohydrates, protein and fats. As well as providing energy in the form of glucose (needed to fuel the body's organs, tissues, brain and muscles), carbohydrates also assist in the absorption of calcium, necessary for good bone health, and help to deliver good intestinal bacteria. There are two main forms: simple carbohydrates (sweets, soft drinks, processed foods and high carb fruits) that break down quickly in the body to form glucose and complex carbohydrates (whole grains and vegetables) which take longer to break down, giving us a feeling of fullness and providing an array of other nutrients our body needs. What is really meant when we talk about a low-carb diet is a diet that is low in refined carbs – limiting foods that contain refined sugar, white flours, or high GI starch; all foods that tend to be highly processed and often high in saturated fats. These are the foods that have poor nutritional merit.

In comparison to a low-fat diet, there's a growing body of evidence showing low-carb diets to be more successful in shifting weight. The theory of a low-carb diet is that by lowering the availability of refined carbohydrates to your body, it is then forced to burn more fat. Secondly that consuming fat slows down digestion – food stays longer in your stomach and takes longer to be broken down and absorbed. This can help you to feel less hungry. Protein also provides an appetite supressing affect resulting in reduced kilojoule intake to elicit weight loss. So switching to a low-carb diet makes it easier to consume less kilojoules without consciously trying to eat less.

WHAT SHOULD YOU BE EATING?

It is important to be aware that there is not one prescription diet for everyone; age, sex, current health and activity levels are all things that have a bearing on your energy requirements and thus the types of food you should be eating. That said, the best diet for any of us is the one that embraces whole food groups, is a balance of lean protein, complex carbs and good fats, and is the one that you feel unburdened by and consequently are likely to stick with long term.

FOODS TO EMBRACE

Carbohydrates choose from wholegrain sources and limit refined ones (such as white flour).

Protein choose lean proteins – free-range chicken and pork, or grass-fed beef. Make sustainable seafood choices concentrating on including oily fish in the mix. Vegetarians can meet their protein needs with: eggs, pulses, soy products, whole unrefined grains, unsweetened full-fat yoghurt, kefir, nuts and seeds.

Vegetables fill your plate (or bowl) with an abundance of colourful vegetables with a mix of less starchy and starch ones in moderation. In general, sweeter dense-fleshed vegetables such as sweet potato tend to be higher in carbs while those from the cabbage family (broccoli, kale, cauliflower, brussels sprout) or those with a high water content are low.

Fruit is sometimes considered the devil of a low-carb diet. However, with a balanced approach it is possible to eat fruit in moderation. Whilst fruit is certainly higher in carbs then non-starchy vegetables, it is considerably lower than bread or pasta, and comes with the added benefits of fibre, vitamins and antioxidants. Most people are able to include some fruit in their day-to-day diets and still adhere to a low-carb diet, depending on their activity levels and weight goals. Before reaching for a banana, it is useful to know that the carb content of fruit varies dramatically. For example, watermelon is one of the lowest carb fruits, while an apple is considered moderate, and a banana high. So depending on your goals you might want to consider – is it better to eat more low-carbs vegies and feel fuller and only occasionally have a piece of fruit?

Nuts and seeds these are particularly useful to include in a vegetarian low-carb diet and, while high in fat, the type of fat is considered beneficial. They're also packed with protein, minerals and other nutrients.

HOW TO MAKE SUCCESSFUL CHANGES

Just as a sedentary lifestyle and a diet that is high in refined carbohydrates can lead to weight gain and poor health, making simple healthy changes to our lifestyle through diet and increased physical activity can lower our risk of many chronic diseases (diabetes, heart disease, even cancer). There is much to be gained from even the smallest of changes.

START SMALL

Making gradual changes to your diet, especially if you are someone who has recognised that a significant reboot is required will allow you to adapt, while simultaneously bolstering your confidence, as the benefit of change starts to kick in. This will help you to maintain this diet long term.

CHANGING HABITS

Cakes, sweets and soft drinks can create a huge carb surplus when we eat them frequently, leading to weight gain and derailing the best intended plan! If you find yourself hooked on 'treats', work on a strategy to decrease the frequency and/or quantities you consume.

Next stage! Swap in healthy snacks (low-carb fruit such as ½ cup berries, a handful of mixed nuts, a boiled egg, hummus and raw vegetables or unsweetened yoghurt). Ultimately, ensure that you are not skipping breakfast and are eating regularly to avoid 3pm slumps and late night nibbles, times of the day when it is easy to bomb with your strategy.

GIVING UP THE FIZZ

Soft drinks in particular can be hard to give up. If you can't go cold turkey, try diluting drinks with mineral water in increasing quantities to accustom your palate to less sugary tastes. Make substitutes by infusing mineral (or still water) with citrus rind, mint sprigs, slices of cucumber or vanilla extract. Teas are also a great go-to with a vast range of tastes. In summer, stock the fridge with jugs of chilled iced tea. In winter, if you feel the need for sugar in your tea, try stevia or switch to a tannin-free herbal infusion.

WHAT ABOUT ALCOHOL?

Most alcoholic beverages are high carb. White wine and spirits are lower carb options than even low-carb beers, if you want to make the best health decision around beer you are better off with a low-alcohol one. Depending on what you want to achieve with your diet, if weight loss is your main goal you will be better off putting your alcohol kilojoules towards food that fuels and nourishes your body.

COOK FOR YOURSELF

Cooking more often for ourselves from scratch with whole foods is one of the simplest and most positive changes we can make to improve our diets. By taking control of what we eat means we can cut out food groups that we don't need.

MENU PREP

When it comes to eating well, preparation is the key to success. Write a weekly meal plan (or see Five Day Dinner Plan, page 11). Weekends are often a great time to get a headstart on the busy week ahead. Consider cooking Mondays' night meal the Sunday before. Create trays with dry goods for each meal of the week, weighing out ingredients if possible. Similarly, organise the fridge for easy access to ingredients. Scour recipes for 'do-ahead' tips; many things such as spiralising vegetables can be done several days in advance; store in airtight bags or containers in the fridge.

ABOUT OUR RECIPES

The meals in this book are based around lean meat, fish and vegetables sources of protein for better health and possibly weight loss. In the long term, some low-carb diets can be lacking in fibre and eating too much protein can put a strain on the kidneys. In our recipes we have balanced meat with plenty of plant-based foods, roughage and complex carbs to aid with satiety, fibre and nutrients to create complete balanced meals.

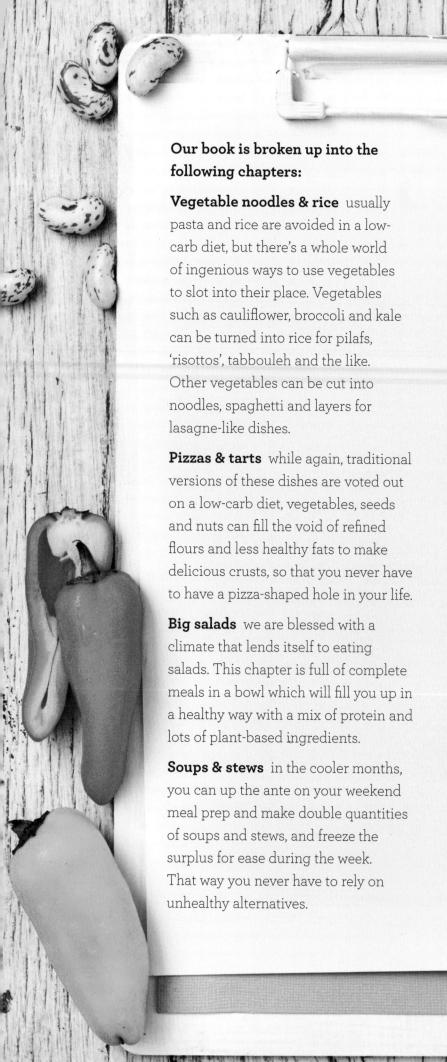

Our book is broken up into the following chapters:

Vegetable noodles & rice usually pasta and rice are avoided in a low-carb diet, but there's a whole world of ingenious ways to use vegetables to slot into their place. Vegetables such as cauliflower, broccoli and kale can be turned into rice for pilafs, 'risottos', tabbouleh and the like. Other vegetables can be cut into noodles, spaghetti and layers for lasagne-like dishes.

Pizzas & tarts while again, traditional versions of these dishes are voted out on a low-carb diet, vegetables, seeds and nuts can fill the void of refined flours and less healthy fats to make delicious crusts, so that you never have to have a pizza-shaped hole in your life.

Big salads we are blessed with a climate that lends itself to eating salads. This chapter is full of complete meals in a bowl which will fill you up in a healthy way with a mix of protein and lots of plant-based ingredients.

Soups & stews in the cooler months, you can up the ante on your weekend meal prep and make double quantities of soups and stews, and freeze the surplus for ease during the week. That way you never have to rely on unhealthy alternatives.

Grills & bakes fire-up the barbecue for fast hitting summer burger and kebab recipes. Hold the bread for those burgers and again look to plant-based options to sandwich your protein between – sweet potato, eggplant and lettuce are all clever options. Or for a feather light bun try our cloud bread (page 179). Winter months see the oven switched on more regularly for cooking roasts and bakes. Even if you are not a vegetarian it is still good to have a meat-free day once or twice a week, try a hearty bake and you won't even feel like you are missing out.

LOW-CARB LIFE

As with any dietary adjustment, if you are pregnant, breast feeding, elderly or ill seek the advice of a medical professional before making changes to your diet. When we cook for ourselves with a balance of whole natural foods without even being conscious of it, we are likely to promote health and wellness. The key to change is to be practical in your approach, if you have been used to eating a certain way for a long time, a sudden change in direction might be hard to adhere to. So make sure you give yourself time to adjust to the changes. Happy cooking and eating, and get your body moving!

FIVE DAY *Dinner Plan*

PLANT-BASED
(FOR WARM DAYS)

Day one Zucchini noodle & kale salad (page 17)

Day two Roast pumpkin with wild mushrooms & pecorino (page 78)

Day three Broccoli rice with chilli & crispy egg (page 21)

Day four Barbecued marinated tofu with chinese broccoli (page 197)

Day five Spring vegetable & labneh tarts (page 69)

KICK START & SHIFT
(FOR COOL DAYS)

Day one Winter tabbouleh with fish (page 38)

Day two Poached chicken salad with winter green salad (page 116)

Day three Jalapeño & roast capsicum beef pot pies (page 92)

Day four One-pan fish arrabbiata (page 201)

Day five Cauliflower tortillas with pulled pork (page 74)

PLANT-BASED
(FOR COOL DAYS)

Day one Bean, silver beet & tomato stew with almond crumble (page 154)

Day two Beetroot & white bean gnocchi with rocket pesto (page 26)

Day three Zucchini & parmesan soup with parmesan crisps (page 149)

Day four Kitchari lentils with spicy cashews (page 41)

Day five Free-form beetroot, goat's cheese hazelnut tart (page 70)

MAINTAIN OR ACTIVE PEOPLE
(FOR WARM DAYS)

Day one Grilled ocean trout with herbed lentils (page 228)

Day two Chicken & lime with daikon noodles (page 29)

Day three Quinoa crisp fattoush with seared lamb (page 119)

Day four Pan-fried fish with wild rice & roast capsicum salad (page 30)

Day five Korean chicken wings with sweet & sour cucumber noodles (page 22)

KICK START & SHIFT
(FOR WARM DAYS)

Day one Roast salmon with spiced cauliflower & spinach (page 136)

Day two: Korean beef salad with kimchi crunch slaw (page 128)

Day three Crisp cauliflower rice with ginger prawns (page 33)

Day four Pork fillet salad with maple miso dressing (page 209)

Day five Wasabi fish burgers in cloud bread buns (page 190)

MAINTAIN OR ACTIVE PEOPLE
(FOR COOL DAYS)

Day one Turkey & kale lasagne (page 48)

Day two Pick-your-protein curry (page 153)

Day three Fennel 'risotto' with smoked trout & charred corn (page 51)

Day four Sweet potato beef nachos (page 124)

Day five Fragrant Vietnamese-style beef stew (page 175)

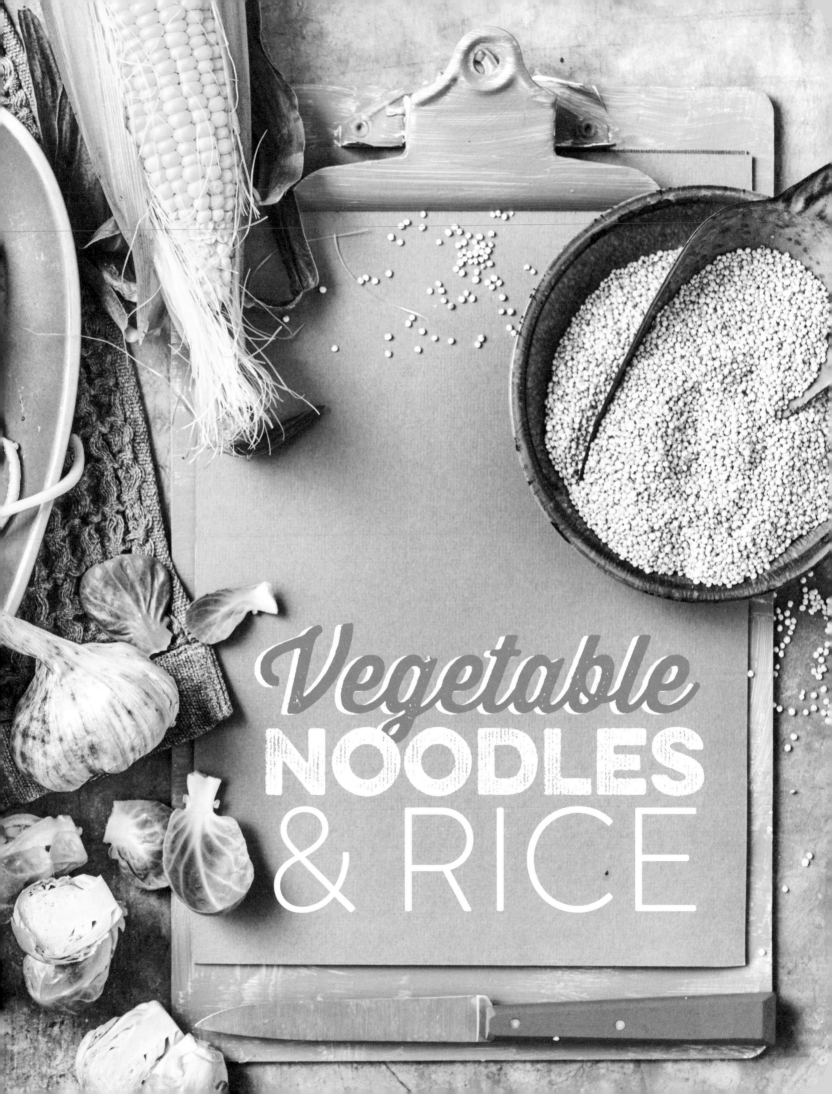

Vegetable
NOODLES
& RICE

CAULIFLOWER SUSHI
WITH SALMON & PICKLED DAIKON

PREP + COOK TIME 50 MINUTES (+ REFRIGERATION) **MAKES** 6 ROLLS

You will need to start this recipe 8 hours ahead.
You will also need a sushi mat.

1KG (2 POUNDS) CAULIFLOWER, CUT INTO FLORETS

2 TABLESPOONS COCONUT OIL

⅓ CUP (80ML) SUSHI SEASONING

300G (9½ OUNCE) PIECE SASHIMI-GRADE SALMON

1 LARGE AVOCADO (320G)

6 NORI (SEAWEED) SHEETS

**6 THIN GREEN ONIONS (SCALLIONS),
GREEN ENDS ONLY**

⅓ CUP (100G) MAYONNAISE

¼ CUP (40G) SESAME SEEDS, TOASTED

2 TABLESPOONS TAMARI

1 TEASPOON WASABI PASTE, APPROXIMATELY

PICKLED PINK GINGER, OPTIONAL

PICKLED DAIKON

1 CUP (250ML) SAKE

1 CUP (250ML) RICE WINE VINEGAR

⅓ CUP (80ML) LIGHT AGAVE SYRUP

2 TEASPOONS SEA SALT FLAKES

**½ SMALL DAIKON (200G), PEELED,
CUT INTO MATCHSTICKS**

1 Make pickled daikon.

2 Process cauliflower, in two batches, until finely chopped and resembles rice. Heat coconut oil in a frying pan over medium-high heat; cook cauliflower, stirring, for 3 minutes or until cooked through – do not brown. Stir in sushi seasoning. Spread onto a large tray; refrigerate for 20 minutes or until cool.

3 Meanwhile, cut salmon into long strips. Cut avocado into thin wedges.

4 Place sushi mat on clean bench. Place a nori sheet close to the bottom edge of the mat. Press one-sixth of the cauliflower firmly onto nori, leaving a 5cm (2-inch) border at the top. Make a slight furrow along the top and bottom of cauliflower to help when rolling. Add one-sixth of the salmon and avocado wedges in a row then a few pieces of green onion, mayonnaise then pickled daikon. Sprinkle over 1 teaspoon of the seeds.

5 To roll, fold over the bottom edge and press to roll up firmly. Wet fingers with cold water and dampen the nori border, then continue rolling to enclose. Roll sushi in mat between your hands a few times to make sure it's well formed. Transfer to a board. Brush top of roll lengthways lightly with a little water; sprinkle with a pinch of the remaining seeds. Wipe mat clean and repeat with remaining cauliflower, salmon, avocado wedges, green onion, mayonnaise, pickled daikon and sesame seeds to make 6 sushi rolls in total.

6 Cut each sushi roll into 5 pieces (don't be tempted to cut it thinner as this will squash the sushi – the cauliflower is not as firm as rice). Serve sushi with tamari, wasabi and pickled ginger.

pickled daikon Combine sake, vinegar, agave syrup and salt in a glass or ceramic bowl. Add daikon. Cover; refrigerate for 8 hours or overnight.

nutritional count per per roll 38g total fat (12g saturated fat); 2452kJ (586 cal); 28g carbohydrate; 18g protein; 6g fibre

tips You can grate the cauliflower if you don't have a food processor. Keep a bowl of ice cold water to dip your hands in while making the sushi; this helps keep the sushi clean and stops the cauliflower sticking to your fingers. You can fill the sushi with your favourite filling ingredients.

do ahead Pickled daikon will keep in the pickling liquid for several weeks. Serve with ramen or in Asian-style salads and with rice.

ZUCCHINI NOODLE & KALE SALAD

PREP TIME 30 MINUTES **SERVES** 4

2 CLOVES GARLIC, CRUSHED

¼ CUP (60ML) KECAP MANIS

2 TEASPOONS SESAME OIL

1 TABLESPOON FINELY GRATED FRESH GINGER

10CM (4-INCH) STALK FRESH LEMON GRASS,
WHITE PART ONLY, CHOPPED FINELY

⅓ CUP (80ML) LIME JUICE

¾ CUP (100G) DRY-ROASTED CASHEWS,
CHOPPED COARSELY

750G (1½ POUNDS) ZUCCHINI

1 LARGE BUNCH GREEN KALE (400G), TRIMMED
(SEE TIPS), LEAVES TORN INTO SMALL PIECES

1 TABLESPOON PEANUT OIL

3 GREEN ONIONS (SCALLIONS),
SLICED THINLY LENGTHWAYS

½ CUP LOOSELY PACKED FRESH MINT LEAVES

1 TABLESPOON WHITE SESAME SEEDS, TOASTED

1 Place garlic, kecap manis, sesame oil, ginger, lemon grass, juice and half the cashews in the bowl of a small food processor; process until well combined.

2 Using a spiraliser (see tips), cut zucchini into thick noodles.

3 Combine kale and peanut oil in a large bowl. Using your hands, massage the oil into the kale to soften. Add zucchini, noodles, half the green onion, half the mint and half the dressing to kale; toss gently to combine.

4 Divide salad among plates; drizzle with remaining dressing. Serve topped with remaining green onion, cashews, mint and the sesame seeds.

nutritional count per serving 24g total fat (4g saturated fat); 1544kJ (369 cal); 25g carbohydrate; 10g protein; 8g fibre

tips Cut out the tough centre vein from each kale leaf and discard it. A spiraliser is a kitchen gadget that cuts vegetables to resemble noodles. If you don't have one, you can use a julienne peeler or a julienne attachment on a mandoline or V-slicer. Recipe is best made close to serving.

PARSNIP NOODLES WITH SPICY LAMB MEATBALL RAGÙ

PREP + COOK TIME 35 MINUTES **SERVES** 4

¼ CUP (60ML) EXTRA VIRGIN OLIVE OIL

600G (1¼ POUNDS) LAMB SAUSAGES

400G (12½ OUNCES) SHALLOTS, CHOPPED FINELY

2 CLOVES GARLIC, CHOPPED FINELY

2 TEASPOONS SMOKED PAPRIKA

1 TEASPOON GROUND CUMIN

1 TEASPOON GROUND CORIANDER

1 TEASPOON FENNEL SEEDS

2 TABLESPOONS FRESH THYME LEAVES

2 TABLESPOONS TOMATO PASTE

1 TABLESPOON HARISSA PASTE

2 CUPS (500ML) CHICKEN STOCK

400G (12½ OUNCES) CANNED DICED TOMATOES

6 LARGE PARSNIPS (2KG), TRIMMED

25G (¾ OUNCE) BUTTER

¼ CUP (20G) FINELY GRATED PECORINO CHEESE

¼ CUP LOOSELY PACKED FRESH OREGANO

1 Heat 1 tablespoon of the oil in a large deep frying pan over medium heat. Squeeze sausage meat from casings, separating into small meatballs; cook meatballs, shaking pan occasionally, for 4 minutes or until browned all over. Remove from pan.

2 Heat another 1 tablespoon of the oil in same pan over medium heat. Cook shallots and garlic, stirring occasionally, for 5 minutes or until softened.

3 Add spices and fennel seeds; cook, stirring, for 1 minute. Add thyme and pastes; cook, stirring, for a further 2 minutes or until fragrant. Stir in stock and tomatoes; bring to the boil. Reduce heat to low; simmer for 10 minutes or until reduced by half. Stir meatballs into sauce. Season to taste. Keep sauce hot over low heat.

4 Using a spiraliser (see tips), cut parsnips into thick noodles. Heat butter and remaining oil in a separate large deep frying pan with a lid, over medium heat. Add parsnip; cook, covered, for 5 minutes or until just tender. Season to taste.

5 Serve parsnip noodles with meatballs and sauce, topped with pecorino and oregano.

nutritional count per serving 45g total fat (15g saturated fat); 3416kJ (816 cal); 50g carbohydrate; 44g protein; 19g fibre

tips A spiraliser is a kitchen gadget that cuts vegetables to resemble noodles. If you don't have one, you can use a julienne peeler or a julienne attachment on a mandoline or V-slicer. Any sausages can be used for this recipe. Sauce makes 4 cups. You can add baby spinach leaves to the sauce.

do-ahead The sauce can be made a day ahead or frozen for up to 2 months. Parsnip noodles are best made just before serving.

BROCCOLI RICE
WITH CHILLI & CRISPY EGG

PREP + COOK TIME 30 MINUTES **SERVES** 4

750G (1½ POUNDS) BROCCOLI

100G (3 OUNCES) SUGAR SNAP PEAS, TRIMMED

100G (3 OUNCES) SNOW PEAS, TRIMMED

¼ CUP (60ML) PEANUT OIL

1 SMALL RED ONION (100G), SLICED THINLY

2 CLOVES GARLIC, CRUSHED

2 TEASPOONS GRATED FRESH GINGER

2 FRESH LONG RED CHILLIES, SLICED THINLY

1 CUP (80G) BEAN SPROUTS

2 TEASPOONS FISH SAUCE

4 EGGS

1 Cut broccoli into florets; coarsely chop stems. Add broccoli florets and stems to a medium saucepan of boiling water; boil for 1 minute. Remove broccoli from the water with a slotted spoon. Place broccoli in a bowl of iced water until cool. Remove from water; drain on a clean tea towel or paper towel. Repeat with sugar snap peas and snow peas, cooking snow peas for 30 seconds. Cut snow peas in half diagonally.

2 Process broccoli stems and florets in a small food processor until finely chopped and resembles rice grains. Transfer to a medium bowl.

3 Heat 2 tablespoons of the oil in a wok or large frying pan over medium-high heat. Stir-fry onion for 3 minutes or until softened. Add garlic, ginger and chilli; stir-fry for 1 minute or until fragrant. Add sugar snap peas and snow peas; stir-fry for 1 minute or until heated through.

4 Add broccoli rice, sprouts and fish sauce to wok; stir-fry for 1 minute or until well combined. Divide broccoli mixture among bowls or plates.

5 Heat 1 teaspoon of the remaining oil in a wok or frying pan; cook 1 egg until white is set and edges are just crisp. Place egg on top of broccoli mixture in bowl. Repeat with remaining oil and eggs.

nutritional count per serving 21g total fat (4g saturated fat); 1214kJ (290 cal); 6g carbohydrate; 15g protein; 7g fibre

tips You can use cauliflower in place of broccoli. Boil cauliflower florets for 2 minutes. If using a large frying pan, cook all the eggs at once. For a vegetarian option, substitute fish sauce with soy sauce.

KOREAN CHICKEN WINGS WITH SWEET & SOUR CUCUMBER NOODLES

PREP + COOK TIME 1 HOUR 20 MINUTES (+ REFRIGERATION & STANDING) **SERVES** 4

1 MEDIUM ONION (150G), GRATED

¼ CUP (80G) GOCHUJANG (SEE TIPS)

2 TABLESPOONS MIRIN

1 TABLESPOON SOY SAUCE

3 CLOVES GARLIC, CRUSHED

1 TEASPOON GRATED FRESH GINGER

1KG (2 POUNDS) CHICKEN WINGS

2 TABLESPOONS PEANUT OIL

2 TEASPOONS BLACK SESAME SEEDS

2 TEASPOONS WHITE SESAME SEEDS, TOASTED

SWEET & SOUR CUCUMBER NOODLES

3 TELEGRAPH (HOTHOUSE) CUCUMBERS (1.2KG), TRIMMED

1 SMALL RED ONION (100G), SLICED THINLY

½ CUP (125ML) RICE WINE VINEGAR

2 TEASPOONS WHITE (GRANULATED) SUGAR

½ TEASPOON CHILLI FLAKES, OPTIONAL

2 TABLESPOONS WATER

1 To make the marinade, combine onion, gochujang, mirin, soy sauce, garlic and ginger in a large bowl.

2 Pat chicken wings dry. Place wings in bowl with marinade; stir to coat. Cover bowl, refrigerate for 4 hours or overnight, stirring occasionally.

3 Meanwhile, make sweet and sour cucumber noodles.

4 Stand wings at room temperature for 30 minutes. Preheat the oven to 200°C/400°F. Line two large oven trays with baking paper.

5 Pour oil over wings in bowl; stir to coat. Divide wings between trays; reserve marinade. Roast wings for 45 minutes, brushing with reserved marinade every 15 minutes, or until wings are browned and cooked through.

6 Transfer drained sweet and sour cucumber noodles to bowls; top with wings and sprinkle with combined sesame seeds.

sweet & sour cucumber noodles Using a julienne attachment on a mandoline or V-slicer, cut cucumber lengthways into long thin strips, until you reach the seeds. Rotate the cucumber a quarter turn and repeat. Continue slicing and rotating the cucumber; discard seeds. Repeat with the remaining cucumbers. Place cucumber noodles in a large bowl. Add the onion, vinegar, sugar, chilli and the water; stir gently. Cover; refrigerate for 2 hours, stirring occasionally.

nutritional count per serving 37g total fat (10g saturated fat); 2389kJ (571 cal); 27g carbohydrate; 29g protein; 5g fibre

tips Gochujang is a Korean chilli paste, available from Asian food stores. For finger food, use chicken wing nibbles (chicken wing pieces) and omit the cucumber noodles.

do-ahead Wings can be refrigerated up to 2 days ahead.

PORK BELLY WITH THAI-STYLE CARROT & ZUCCHINI SALAD

PREP + COOK TIME 2 HOURS 15 MINUTES (+ REFRIGERATION) **SERVES** 4

1KG (2 POUNDS) BONELESS PORK BELLY

1 TABLESPOON EXTRA VIRGIN OLIVE OIL

1 TABLESPOON FINE SEA SALT

1 MEDIUM LEMON (140G), SLICED

2 STEMS FRESH LEMON GRASS (60G), BRUISED, CUT INTO 5CM (2-INCH) LENGTHS

1 TABLESPOON JASMINE RICE

1 MEDIUM LIME (90G), CUT INTO CHEEKS

THAI-STYLE CARROT & ZUCCHINI SALAD

¼ CUP (60ML) LIME JUICE

2 TABLESPOONS FISH SAUCE

1 TEASPOON SESAME OIL

2 TEASPOONS FINELY GRATED PALM SUGAR

1 CLOVE GARLIC, CRUSHED

1 FRESH LONG RED CHILLI, CHOPPED FINELY

3 MEDIUM ZUCCHINI (360G)

1 LARGE CARROT (180G)

¼ CUP LOOSELY PACKED FRESH THAI BASIL LEAVES

¼ CUP LOOSELY PACKED FRESH CORIANDER (CILANTRO) LEAVES

¼ CUP LOOSELY PACKED FRESH MINT LEAVES

1 Preheat oven to 180°C/350°F.

2 Using a small very sharp knife, score the pork skin at 1cm (½-inch) intervals. Pat the pork dry with paper towel. Rub the rind and the cuts with oil then salt. Place the pork, rind-side down, in a shallow-sided heavy-based baking dish.

3 Roast pork for 1½ hours. Increase oven temperature to 220°C/425°F. Working quickly, drain away any excess fat; place lemon and lemon grass next to pork on oven tray. Turn pork, skin-side up, onto the lemon mixture. Roast for a further 30 minutes or until the rind is crisp and pork is tender.

4 Meanwhile, heat a small saucepan or wok over high heat. Add rice; reduce heat to low. Toast rice, stirring constantly, until golden. Transfer rice to a mortar. Twist the pestle, rather than pound, to crush the rice more evenly.

5 Make Thai-style carrot and zucchini salad.

6 Sprinkle salad with roasted rice. Serve salad with sliced pork belly, lime cheeks and remaining dressing.

Thai-style carrot & zucchini salad Stir juice, sauce, oil, sugar, garlic and chilli in a jug until sugar dissolves. Use a julienne attachment on a mandoline or V-slicer, or a spiraliser to cut zucchini and carrots into 5mm (¼-inch) thick long strips. Just before serving, place vegetables in a large bowl; stir through enough dressing to coat. Gently stir in herbs. Place remaining dressing in a small bowl.

nutritional count per serving 140g total fat (48g saturated fat); 5898kJ (1410 cal); 14g carbohydrate; 24g protein; 5g fibre

tips Ask your butcher to score the rind. You could also use a clean cardboard cutter (Stanley knife) to slice the rind. The rind of the pork will crackle better if you leave it uncovered in the fridge for 3 hours or overnight. For super-crispy pork and crackling, a dark coated, heavy-based roasting pan gives a better result.

do-ahead The dressing can be made a day ahead.

BEETROOT & WHITE BEAN GNOCCHI WITH ROCKET PESTO

PREP + COOK TIME 1 HOUR 15 MINUTES (+ REFRIGERATION) **SERVES** 4

1 TABLESPOON EXTRA VIRGIN OLIVE OIL

250G (8 OUNCES) BEETROOT (BEETS), PEELED, GRATED COARSELY

400G (12½ OUNCES) CANNED BUTTER BEANS (LIMA BEANS), DRAINED, RINSED

1 EGG, BEATEN LIGHTLY

½ CUP (40G) FINELY GRATED PARMESAN

½ CUP (85G) FINE SEMOLINA, PLUS EXTRA, TO DUST

40G (1½ OUNCES) BUTTER

¼ CUP (25G) COARSELY CHOPPED WALNUTS, TOASTED

1 CUP (50G) FIRMLY PACKED BABY ROCKET LEAVES

ROCKET PESTO

½ CUP FIRMLY PACKED BABY ROCKET LEAVES

½ CUP FIRMLY PACKED FRESH BASIL LEAVES

⅓ CUP (35G) COARSELY CHOPPED WALNUTS, TOASTED

⅓ CUP (25G) FINELY GRATED PARMESAN

1 CLOVE GARLIC, CRUSHED

¼ CUP (60ML) EXTRA VIRGIN OLIVE OIL

1 TABLESPOON FRESH LEMON JUICE

1 Heat oil in a large frying pan over low heat. Cook beetroot, stirring, for 10 minutes or until soft. Blend or process beetroot with the butter beans until smooth. Season to taste.

2 Place beetroot mixture in a large bowl. Stir in egg, 2 tablespoons of the parmesan and the semolina until a soft, sticky dough is formed.

3 Divide dough into four portions; roll each portion, on a surface dusted with a little extra semolina, into long ropes, about 2cm (¾-inch) thick. Cut each rope into 1cm (½-inch) pieces. Roll pieces into balls then run each piece of dough over the back of a fork to create light indents (this will help the sauce cling to the gnocchi). Place gnocchi, in a single layer, on a semolina-dusted tray. Cover; refrigerate for 1 hour.

4 Meanwhile, make rocket pesto.

5 Cook gnocchi, in batches, in a large saucepan of boiling salted water until gnocchi float to the surface and are cooked through. Remove from pan with a slotted spoon; place in a large shallow bowl. Cover to keep warm. Reserve 2 tablespoons of the cooking water.

6 Melt butter in a large frying pan over high heat. Add cooked gnocchi; stir to combine. Stir the reserved cooking water into the pesto.

7 Divide gnocchi mixture among bowls. Spoon over pesto. Top with walnuts, rocket and remaining parmesan; drizzle with walnut oil.

rocket pesto Blend or process all ingredients until smooth. Season to taste.

nutritional count per serving 47g total fat (13g saturated fat); 2859kJ (683 cal); 41g carbohydrate; 20g protein; 9g fibre

tip The gnocchi dough will be very sticky.

do-ahead Gnocchi can be made to the end of step 3 up to a day ahead; keep refrigerated. Pesto, without the lemon juice, keeps in an airtight container, covered with a thin layer of olive oil in the fridge for up to 1 week or freeze, for up to 1 month. Add the lemon juice just before using.

CHICKEN & LIME
WITH DAIKON NOODLES

PREP + COOK TIME 25 MINUTES **SERVES** 2

1 MEDIUM DAIKON (600G)

1 TABLESPOON VEGETABLE OIL

4 CHICKEN THIGH FILLETS (680G), SLICED

4 GREEN ONIONS (SCALLIONS), SLICED

1 MEDIUM CARROT (120G), SLICED THINLY

¼ CUP (60ML) FRESH LIME JUICE

2 TABLESPOONS LIGHT SOY SAUCE

1 TABLESPOON HONEY

1 FRESH LONG RED CHILLI, CHOPPED FINELY

½ CUP LOOSELY PACKED FRESH CORIANDER (CILANTRO) LEAVES

2 TABLESPOONS COARSELY CHOPPED PEANUTS

1 Using a julienne peeler or spiraliser, cut daikon into long thin strips.

2 Heat the oil in a large wok or frying pan over high heat. Stir-fry the chicken, in batches, until browned. Reserve. Stir-fry the green onion and carrot until just tender. Return chicken to wok.

3 Meanwhile, combine lime juice, soy sauce, honey and chilli in a small bowl. Add juice mixture to the wok with daikon noodles. Stir-fry for 3 minutes or until chicken is cooked through.

4 Serve chicken noodle mixture sprinkled with coriander leaves and peanuts.

nutritional count per serving 45g total fat (11g saturated fat); 3227kJ (771 cal); 21g carbohydrate; 66g protein; 10g fibre

tip For a vegan version of this recipe, use chopped firm tofu instead of chicken.

PAN-FRIED FISH WITH WILD RICE & ROAST CAPSICUM SALAD

PREP + COOK TIME 55 MINUTES **SERVES** 4

¼ CUP (50G) WILD RICE

2 MEDIUM RED CAPSICUMS (BELL PEPPERS) (400G)

2 CELERY STALKS (300G), SLICED THINLY, LEAVES RESERVED

½ MEDIUM RED ONION (85G), SLICED THINLY

250G (8 OUNCES) CHERRY TOMATOES, CUT INTO WEDGES

1 TEASPOON POMEGRANATE MOLASSES

1 TEASPOON RED WINE VINEGAR

¼ CUP (60ML) OLIVE OIL

⅔ CUP (80G) ALMOND MEAL

2 TABLESPOONS CHOPPED FRESH DILL

8 THIN WHITE FISH FILLETS (960G)

50G (1½ OUNCES) BUTTER

1 Bring a medium saucepan of salted water to the boil. Add wild rice; simmer, uncovered, for 40 minutes or until tender. Drain; rinse under cold water. Drain well. Transfer wild rice to a large bowl.

2 Meanwhile, quarter capsicum; discard seeds and membranes. Roast, skin-side up, under a hot grill (broiler) or in a very hot oven, until skin blisters and blackens. Cover capsicum for 5 minutes, peel away skin; chop coarsely.

3 Reserve 1 cup of the young pale celery leaves from the centre of the celery bunch. Add celery leaves, sliced celery, capsicum, onion and tomato to wild rice; mix gently.

4 To make the dressing, place molasses, vinegar and oil in a small jug or bowl; stir to combine. Season to taste.

5 Combine almond meal and dill in a large shallow bowl; season. Coat fillets in almond meal mixture. Heat half the butter in a large non-stick frying pan. When butter is starting to foam, add the fillets. Cook fillets, in two batches, with remaining butter, for 2 minutes each side or until lightly golden and just cooked through.

6 Add the dressing to the wild rice mixture; toss gently. Season to taste. Serve fish fillets with the wild rice salad.

nutritional count per serving 39g total fat (10g saturated fat); 2740kJ (655 cal); 17g carbohydrate; 56g protein; 6g fibre

tips We used whiting fillets in this recipe but any white fish fillets will be fine. Cooking time of the fish will depend on the thickness. You will need to buy at least half a bunch of celery for the leaves.

serving suggestion Serve with a leafy green salad.

CRISP CAULIFLOWER RICE WITH GINGER PRAWNS

PREP + COOK TIME 1 HOUR **SERVES** 4

900G (1¾ POUNDS) CAULIFLOWER FLORETS

4 FRESH LONG GREEN CHILLIES (40G), SEEDED, SLICED THINLY

24 LARGE UNCOOKED KING PRAWNS (1.68KG)

1 BUNCH FRESH CORIANDER (CILANTRO) (100G)

1 TABLESPOON GRATED FRESH GINGER

1 TABLESPOON FINELY CHOPPED FRESH LEMON GRASS

1 TEASPOON FINELY GRATED LIME RIND

2 TABLESPOONS FRESH LIME JUICE

2 TABLESPOONS EXTRA VIRGIN OLIVE OIL

4 GREEN ONIONS (SCALLIONS), SLICED THINLY

1 CUP (160G) UNSALTED ROASTED CASHEWS

2 TABLESPOONS SESAME SEEDS, TOASTED

1 MEDIUM LIME (90G), CUT INTO WEDGES

1 Preheat oven to 180°C/350°F. Line two large baking dishes with baking paper.

2 Process cauliflower until finely chopped and resembles rice grains. Transfer cauliflower to a large bowl; season. Stir in chilli. Spread evenly into baking dishes.

3 Roast cauliflower for 40 minutes or until browned and tender, stirring occasionally.

4 Meanwhile, shell and devein prawns, leaving tails intact. Wash coriander well; trim coriander roots. Finely chop roots and stems; place in a medium bowl. Reserve coriander leaves. Add ginger, lemon grass, rind, juice and oil; mix well. Add the prawns; stir to coat. Cover; refrigerate for 30 minutes.

5 Cook prawns in two batches in a heated oiled frying pan or grill pan (or barbecue) for 2 minutes each side or until changed in colour and just cooked through.

6 Stir green onion, cashews and seeds into cauliflower; season to taste. Serve cauliflower mixture topped with prawns, reserved coriander leaves and lime wedges.

nutritional count per serving 36g total fat (6g saturated fat); 2701kJ (646 cal); 16g carbohydrate; 58g protein; 13g fibre

serving suggestion The cauliflower rice can also be served as a side in place of rice or couscous to accompany grilled fish, curries, casseroles or tagines.

CREAMY BACON PUMPKIN SPAGHETTI

PREP + COOK TIME 30 MINUTES **SERVES** 4

1.5KG (3 POUNDS) BUTTERNUT PUMPKIN, PEELED

2 TABLESPOONS EXTRA VIRGIN OLIVE OIL

½ CUP (55G) COARSELY CHOPPED WALNUTS

2 TABLESPOONS PEPITAS (PUMPKIN SEED KERNELS)

4 SLICES BACON (260G), TRIMMED, CHOPPED

⅔ CUP (160ML) POURING CREAM

⅔ CUP (160ML) MILK

¾ CUP (60G) FINELY GRATED PECORINO CHEESE

1 TABLESPOON CHOPPED FRESH CHIVES

1 Preheat oven to 200°C/400°F. Line three oven trays with baking paper.

2 Using a spiraliser or julienne attachment on a mandoline or V-slicer, cut pumpkin into long thin strips (see tips). Combine pumpkin and oil in a large bowl; season.

3 Spread pumpkin srtips in a single layer between two trays. Roast for 12 minutes or until just tender; cover to keep warm. If using thinner noodles, you will need to reduce the cooking time. Meanwhile, place walnuts and pepitas on the third tray; roast for 5 minutes or until fragrant.

4 Cook bacon in a medium frying pan over medium heat, stirring occasionally, for 5 minutes or until browned. Add cream, milk and ½ cup of the pecorino; bring to the boil. Simmer for 5 minutes or until sauce thickens. Season to taste.

5 Carefully transfer pumpkin to a large shallow bowl. Pour sauce over pumpkin; top with roasted nut mixture, remaining pecorino and chives. Season with freshly ground black pepper. Serve immediately.

nutritional count per serving 48g total fat (17g saturated fat); 2675kJ (639 cal); 25g carbohydrate; 25g protein; 7g fibre

tips We found the spiraliser gave the best results; a julienne peeler makes fine strips which break down when cooked. For a shortcut, you can also purchase 1.2kg (2½ pounds) pumpkin noodles from some greengrocers. You can try this with sweet potato or parsnip instead of pumpkin. This recipe is best made just before serving.

KELP NOODLES
WITH PEANUT PRAWNS

PREP + COOK TIME 35 MINUTES **SERVES** 4

½ CUP (75G) ROASTED SALTED PEANUTS

1 SHEET NORI (SEAWEED), CHOPPED COARSELY

2 TABLESPOONS SESAME SEEDS

1KG (2 POUNDS) UNCOOKED KING PRAWNS

2 EGG WHITES, BEATEN LIGHTLY

400G (12½ OUNCES) KELP NOODLES

2 TABLESPOONS FISH SAUCE

2 TABLESPOONS BROWN RICE SYRUP

¼ CUP (60ML) LIME JUICE

3 CUPS (240G) FINELY SHREDDED RED CABBAGE

3 CUPS (240G) FINELY SHREDDED WOMBOK

2 FRESH LONG RED CHILLIES, SEEDED,
CUT INTO LONG THIN STRIPS

1 CUP LOOSELY PACKED FRESH CORIANDER
(CILANTRO) LEAVES

1 LITRE (4 CUPS) PEANUT OIL, FOR DEEP-FRYING

1 MEDIUM LIME (90G), CUT INTO WEDGES

1 Pulse peanuts and nori in a small food processor until a semi-coarse crumble forms. Stir in sesame seeds. Shell and devein prawns, leaving tails intact. Combine prawns and egg white in a medium bowl. Press peanut crumble around prawns, except the tails.

2 Place noodles in a large bowl; cover with warm water. Stand for 10 minutes.

3 Meanwhile, to make dressing, combine fish sauce, syrup and juice in a jug. Drain noodles; return to bowl. Pour dressing over noodles, mix gently. Add red cabbage, wombok, chilli and half the coriander to noodles; toss well.

4 Heat oil in a small wok or medium saucepan; deep-fry prawns, in batches, for 1 minute or until changed in colour and just cooked through. Drain prawns on paper towel.

5 Serve noodle mixture topped with prawns, remaining coriander and the lime wedges.

nutritional count per serving 30g total fat (5g saturated fat); 2109kJ (504 cal); 15g carbohydrate; 37g protein; 8g fibre
tip You will need to buy about ½ small red cabbage for the amount of shredded cabbage in this recipe.
do-ahead Dressing can be made up to 2 days ahead; keep covered in the fridge.

WINTER TABBOULEH WITH FISH

PREP + COOK TIME 30 MINUTES **SERVES** 4

1 LARGE HEAD BROCCOLI WITH STEMS (400G),
CHOPPED COARSELY

3 MEDIUM ROMA (PLUM) TOMATOES (180G),
CHOPPED FINELY

1 LEBANESE CUCUMBER (130G), PEELED,
CHOPPED FINELY

3 GREEN ONIONS (SCALLIONS) (75G),
CHOPPED FINELY

1 CUP LOOSELY PACKED FRESH FLAT-LEAF
PARSLEY LEAVES, CHOPPED FINELY

1½ CUPS LOOSELY PACKED FRESH MINT LEAVES,
CHOPPED FINELY

PINCH GROUND ALLSPICE

PINCH GROUND CINNAMON

¼ CUP (60ML) FRESH LIME JUICE

¼ CUP (60ML) EXTRA VIRGIN OLIVE OIL

4 X 200G (6½-OUNCE) SKINLESS FIRM WHITE
FISH FILLETS, HALVED

1 CLOVE GARLIC, CRUSHED

⅓ CUP (65G) PEPITAS (PUMPKIN SEED KERNELS)

1 SMALL LIME (65G), CUT INTO CHEEKS

1 Process the broccoli including the stems until finely chopped. Transfer to a large bowl. Stir in tomato, cucumber, green onion, parsley and mint.

2 To make the dressing, combine the allspice, cinnamon, lime juice and half the oil in a small bowl; season to taste. Drizzle dressing over salad.

3 Rub fish with garlic; season. Heat the remaining oil in a large frying pan over medium heat. Cook fish, in batches, for 4 minutes each side or until just cooked through. Add pepitas to the pan for the last 2 minutes; cook, stirring occasionally, until toasted lightly.

4 Divide salad between bowls. Top with fish and pepitas; serve with lime cheeks.

nutritional count per serving 27g total fat (5g saturated fat); 1981kJ (473 cal); 4g carbohydrate; 49g protein; 6g fibre

tips We used blue eye travalla in this recipe, but any white fish fillet will be fine. Cooking time of the fish fillets will depend on the thickness.

do-ahead The salad can be made to the end of step 1, and the dressing can be made up to 8 hours ahead. Keep covered in the fridge.

serving suggestion You could serve this salad with grilled chicken or falafel instead of fish.

KITCHARI LENTILS
WITH SPICY CASHEWS

PREP + COOK TIME 40 MINUTES **SERVES** 4

400G (12½ OUNCES) BROCCOLI

2 TABLESPOONS EXTRA VIRGIN OLIVE OIL

2 MEDIUM RED ONIONS (340G), SLICED THINLY

2 CLOVES GARLIC, CRUSHED

1 TEASPOON GARAM MASALA

1 TEASPOON YELLOW MUSTARD SEEDS

2 SPRIGS CURRY LEAVES (AROUND 18 LEAVES)

1 CUP (200G) FRENCH-STYLE GREEN LENTILS

2½ CUPS (625ML) VEGETABLE STOCK

120G (4 OUNCES) KALE, LEAVES TORN COARSELY

2 BABY CUCUMBERS (60G)

2 TEASPOONS RICE WINE VINEGAR

½ CUP (140G) GREEK-STYLE YOGHURT

SPICY CASHEWS

1 CUP (150G) RAW UNSALTED CASHEWS

2 TEASPOONS EXTRA VIRGIN OLIVE OIL

1 TEASPOON DRIED CHILLI FLAKES

½ TEASPOON SEA SALT FLAKES

1 Make spicy cashews.

2 Meanwhile, cut small florets from the broccoli. Finely chop or process stems.

3 Heat oil in a large deep-sided frying pan over high heat. Add three-quarters of the onion and the garlic; reduce heat to low. Cook covered, stirring occasionally, for 15 minutes or until onion is soft and starting to caramelise.

4 Increase heat to high. Push onion to one side of the pan. Add garam masala, mustard seeds and curry leaves to pan; cook, stirring, for 1 minute or until spices are fragrant and mustard seeds are beginning to pop. Add lentils and stock; stir to combine. Bring to the boil. Reduce heat to a simmer; cook, stirring occasionally, for 15 minutes or until lentils are just tender. Stir in kale and broccoli florets and stems; season to taste. Cover to keep warm.

5 Using a vegetable peeler, peel cucumber into thin ribbons. Combine cucumber, remaining onion and the vinegar in a small bowl; stand for 5 minutes, drain. Season to taste.

6 Serve kitchari topped with cucumber mixture, spicy cashews and yoghurt.

spicy cashews Preheat oven to 180°C/350°F. Line a large oven tray with baking paper. Combine ingredients in a medium bowl. Spread mixture evenly over tray. Roast for 5 minutes, turning halfway through cooking time, or until golden. Cool.

nutritional count per serving 35g total fat (6g saturated fat); 2579kJ (616 cal); 42g carbohydrate; 26g protein; 14g fibre

do-ahead Spicy cashews can be made a week ahead; store in an airtight container. Recipe can be made to the end of step 4 a day ahead.

PARSNIP "PENNE" & CHICKEN SALAD

PREP + COOK TIME 25 MINUTES **SERVES** 4

⅓ CUP (80ML) EXTRA VIRGIN OLIVE OIL

1 TEASPOON FINELY GRATED LEMON RIND

¼ CUP (60ML) FRESH LEMON JUICE

2 TABLESPOONS FINELY CHOPPED FRESH
FLAT-LEAF PARSLEY

½ CUP (60G) PECANS

300G (9½ OUNCES) SHREDDED COOKED CHICKEN

60G (2 OUNCES) BABY ROCKET LEAVES

250G (8 OUNCES) BABY ROMA TOMATOES, HALVED

1 LITRE (4 CUPS) VEGETABLE STOCK

6 MEDIUM PARSNIPS (1.5KG)

2 TEASPOONS FINELY GRATED LEMON RIND, EXTRA

⅓ CUP (25G) FLAKED PARMESAN

1 To make dressing, place oil, rind, juice and half the parsley in a screw-top jar. Shake well; season to taste.

2 Stir pecans in a small heavy-based frying pan over medium heat for 5 minutes or until light golden; transfer to a board. Cool; chop coarsely. Combine pecans, chicken, rocket and tomato in a large bowl.

3 Bring stock to the boil in a medium saucepan. Peel parsnips; cut into 1cm (½-inch) batons. Cut on an angle into 5cm (2-inch) lengths to resemble penne pasta. Cook parsnip in boiling stock for 3 minutes or until tender. Drain parsnip over a heatproof large jug or bowl; reserve stock for another use (see tip).

4 Add parsnip and dressing to chicken mixture; toss well. Season to taste. Top with extra rind, the parmesan and remaining parsley. Serve immediately.

nutritional count per serving 39g total fat (6g saturated fat); 2659kJ (635 cal); 34g carbohydrate; 31g protein; 14g fibre

tip Use leftover vegetable stock in a soup, casserole or sauce.

PUTTANESCA WITH SPAGHETTI SQUASH

PREP + COOK TIME 50 MINUTES **SERVES** 4

2KG (4 POUNDS) SPAGHETTI SQUASH

2 TABLESPOONS EXTRA VIRGIN OLIVE OIL

½ CUP FINELY GRATED PARMESAN

½ CUP FIRMLY PACKED FRESH BASIL LEAVES

PUTTANESCA SAUCE

2 TABLESPOONS OLIVE OIL

1 MEDIUM RED ONION (170G), SLICED THINLY

3 CLOVES GARLIC, SLICED THINLY

4 ANCHOVY FILLETS, CHOPPED FINELY

½ CUP (80G) PITTED KALAMATA OLIVES, TORN COARSELY

1½ TABLESPOONS BABY CAPERS

400G (12½ OUNCES) BUTTER BEANS (LIMA BEANS), DRAINED, RINSED

400G (12½ OUNCES) CHERRY TRUSS TOMATOES

1 FRESH LONG RED CHILLI, SEEDED, SLICED THINLY

1 Preheat oven to 180°C/350°F. Line two oven trays with baking paper.

2 Cut squash in half lengthways; scoop out seeds. Cut squash in half crossways. Place cut-side up on trays. Drizzle with oil; season.

3 Roast squash for 35 minutes or until softened and flesh is just pulling away from the skin.

4 Meanwhile, make puttanesca sauce.

5 Remove flesh from squash and pull apart to form pasta-like strands. Serve spaghetti squash immediately with puttanesca sauce. Top with parmesan and basil.

puttanesca sauce Heat the oil in a large frying pan over medium heat. Cook onion, garlic and anchovies, stirring, for 5 minutes or until onion is soft. Stir in olives, capers, beans and tomatoes; reduce heat to low. Cook, covered, for 15 minutes or until the tomatoes are collapsing; press tomatoes with the back of a spoon to break down. Stir in chilli. Season to taste.

nutritional count per serving 28g total fat (4g saturated fat); 1986kJ (475 cal); 47g carbohydrate; 10g protein; 12g fibre

tips We prefer to use hands to pull apart the spaghetti squash, as a fork will tear it into short pieces. You can use a can of cherry tomatoes instead of the fresh tomatoes, if you prefer.

do-ahead Sauce can be made several hours ahead; add basil just before serving.

serving suggestion Serve with a rocket salad.

spicy lamb meatball ragù

caper & vongole

puttanesca sauce

eggplant & tomato

walnut & almond pesto

creamy bacon & pecorino

Chunky pasta sauces

For these sauces, serve with 800g (1½ pounds) cooked spiralised vegetable of your choice.

SPICY LAMB MEATBALL RAGÙ

prep + cook time 30 minutes **serves** 4

Heat 1 tablespoon olive oil in a large frying pan over medium heat. Squeeze meat from casings of 600g (1¼lbs) lamb sausages; shape into small meatballs. Cook, stirring, 4 minutes until browned. Remove from pan. Heat 1 tablespoon olive oil in same pan over medium heat; cook 2 finely chopped medium (340g) onions and 2 cloves crushed garlic, stirring, for 5 minutes or until soft. Add 2 tablespoons fresh thyme leaves, 2 tablespoons tomato paste, 1 tablespoon harissa and 1 teaspoon each smoked paprika, ground cumin, ground coriander and fennel seeds; cook, stirring, for 3 minutes. Stir in 2 cups chicken stock and 400g (12½oz) canned diced tomatoes; simmer for 10 minutes, until reduced by half. Stir in meatballs until warmed through. Season to taste. Top with ¼ cup grated pecorino.

CAPER & VONGOLE

prep + cook time 15 minutes **serves** 4

Heat 1 tablespoon olive oil in a large saucepan over medium-high heat. Cook 3 crushed cloves garlic and 1 thinly sliced fresh long red chilli, stirring, 1 minute or until garlic is fragrant. Add 1 tablespoon baby capers, ⅓ cup dry white wine and 2 tablespoons lemon juice; bring to the boil. Add 1kg (2lb) vongole (or clams or pipis) and 2 tablespoons chopped fresh lemon thyme. Cook, covered, 5 minutes or until vongole open. Sprinkle with ⅓ cup chopped fresh flat-leaf parsley; drizzle with an extra 2 tablespoons olive oil. Season to taste.

WALNUT & ALMOND PESTO

prep time 10 minutes **serves** 4

Blend or process 2 chopped cloves garlic, ¼ cup each of roasted walnuts and almonds, ½ cup finely grated parmesan and 2 cups firmly packed fresh basil leaves until almost smooth. Gradually add ½ cup extra virgin olive oil in a thin, steady steam, processing until combined. Season to taste.

PUTTANESCA SAUCE

prep + cook time 20 minutes **serves** 4

Heat 2 tablespoons extra virgin oil in a large frying pan over medium heat. Cook 1 medium (170g) thinly sliced red onion, 3 cloves thinly sliced garlic and 4 chopped anchovy fillets, stirring, for 5 minutes or until onion is soft. Stir in ½ cup (60g) pitted, halved kalamata olives, 1½ tablespoons baby capers, 400g (12½oz) canned butter beans and 400g (12½oz) cherry truss tomatoes; reduce heat to low. Cook, covered, for 8 minutes or until the tomatoes are soft. Crush tomatoes with the back of a spoon. Stir in 1 fresh long red chilli, seeded and sliced thinly and ½ cup firmly packed fresh basil leaves, torn. Season.

tip You can use a can of cherry tomatoes instead of the fresh tomatoes, if you prefer.

EGGPLANT & TOMATO

prep + cook time 30 minutes **serves** 4

Heat ¼ cup olive oil in a large frying pan over medium-high heat. Cook 1 medium (150g) finely chopped onion, 2 (200g) finely chopped celery stalks and 1 crushed clove garlic. Cook, stirring, for 5 minutes. Add 1 medium (300g) chopped eggplant; cook, stirring, for 3 minutes or until golden. Add 2 cups tomato passata and ⅓ cup water; bring to the boil. Simmer for 5 minutes. Sprinkle with ¼ cup fresh parsley or basil leaves. Season to taste.

CREAMY BACON & PECORINO

prep + cook time 35 minutes **serves** 4

Preheat oven to 200°C/400°F. Place ½ cup coarsely chopped walnuts and 2 tablespoons pepitas (pumpkin seed kernels) on an oven tray; roast 5 minutes. Meanwhile, cook 4 (260g) trimmed, coarsely chopped bacon slices in a large frying pan for 5 minutes, stirring occasionally, or until browned. Add ⅔ cup pouring cream, ⅔ cup milk and ½ cup finely grated pecorino or parmesan. Bring to the boil; simmer for 5 minutes or until sauce thickens. Season. Serve sprinkled with roasted nut mixture and top with ¼ cup shaved pecorino or extra parmesan.

TURKEY & KALE LASAGNE

PREP + COOK TIME 1 HOUR 25 MINUTES **SERVES** 4

300G (9½ OUNCES) KALE

2 TABLESPOONS EXTRA VIRGIN OLIVE OIL

500G (1 POUND) MINCED (GROUND) TURKEY

1 MEDIUM RED ONION (170G), CHOPPED FINELY

1 MEDIUM CARROT (120G), GRATED FINELY

2 CLOVES GARLIC, CRUSHED

1 TABLESPOON FINELY CHOPPED FRESH ROSEMARY LEAVES

¼ CUP (70G) TOMATO PASTE

400G (12½ OUNCES) CANNED DICED TOMATOES

¾ CUP (75G) GRATED MOZZARELLA

COTTAGE CHEESE SAUCE

750G (1½ POUNDS) COTTAGE CHEESE

½ CUP (40G) FINELY GRATED PARMESAN

1 EGG

1 Preheat oven to 200°C/400°F. Lightly grease a 2.5-litre (10-cup) ovenproof dish.

2 Separate the kale leaves and stems; finely chop the stems, reserve leaves. Heat the oil in a large, deep frying pan over high heat. Cook the kale stems, turkey, onion, carrot, garlic and rosemary, breaking up any lumps with a wooden spoon, for 10 minutes or until browned. Add the paste and diced tomatoes; cook, stirring, for 2 minutes. Season to taste.

3 Meanwhile, drop the kale leaves into a large saucepan of boiling water for 30 seconds; drain. Refresh in a bowl of iced water or under cold water; drain well. Place in a clean tea towel and gently squeeze to remove any excess liquid.

4 Make cottage cheese sauce.

5 Place half the kale leaves across the base of the dish in one layer. Top with half the turkey mixture and half the cottage cheese sauce. Repeat layers. Sprinkle with mozzarella.

6 Bake lasagne for 40 minutes or until top is golden. Stand for 10 minutes before serving.

cottage cheese sauce Whisk all ingredients in a large bowl until combined; season.

nutritional count per serving 34g total fat (14g saturated fat); 2770kJ (662 cal); 14g carbohydrate; 69g protein; 6g fibre

tip You will need one bunch of kale for this recipe. You can also use cavolo nero or silver beet, if you prefer.

do-ahead You can assemble the lasagne several hours ahead. Cover and refrigerate until ready to cook. Add about 10 minutes to the cooking time if baking from cold. Cover the top loosely with a sheet of baking paper or oiled foil if the lasagna is over-browning.

FENNEL "RISOTTO" WITH SMOKED TROUT & CHARRED CORN

PREP + COOK TIME 1 HOUR (+ STANDING) **SERVES** 4

2 CORN COBS (500G), HUSK AND SILK REMOVED

COOKING OIL SPRAY

3 LARGE FENNEL (1.5KG)

1 LITRE (4 CUPS) FISH STOCK

50G (1½ OUNCES) BUTTER

1 LARGE ONION (200G), CHOPPED FINELY

3 CLOVES GARLIC, CHOPPED FINELY

½ CUP (125ML) WHITE WINE

3 EGG YOLKS

1 TABLESPOON THICKENED (HEAVY) CREAM

1 CUP (80G) GRATED PARMESAN

1 TEASPOON FINELY GRATED LEMON RIND

350G (11 OUNCES) WHOLE HOT-SMOKED TROUT, FLESH FLAKED

1 Spray corn cobs with oil. Cook corn on heated barbecue (or grill plate) over high heat for 12 minutes, turning occasionally, or until kernels are slightly charred and tender. When cool enough to handle, cut kernels from cobs.

2 Meanwhile, reserve fronds from fennel. Trim fennel; chop coarsely. Process fennel using the pulse button about 10 times, or until fennel resembles grains of rice.

3 Bring stock to a simmer in a medium saucepan. Melt butter in a deep large frying pan over a medium heat. Cook onion and garlic, stirring, for 4 minutes or until lightly golden. Add fennel; cook, stirring, for 4 minutes or until starting to soften. Add wine; simmer for 1 minute or until evaporated.

4 Add the hot stock to the frying pan; bring to the boil. Reduce heat to medium; simmer for 25 minutes or until fennel is tender. Stir in corn kernels.

5 Combine egg yolks and cream in a small bowl. Stir egg yolk mixture, parmesan and rind into risotto; remove from heat. Season to taste. Place flaked trout on top; cover with a lid, stand for 2 minutes or until heated through.

6 Serve risotto topped with reserved fennel fronds.

nutritional count per serving 27g total fat (14g saturated fat); 2001kJ (478 cal); 19g carbohydrate; 30g protein; 9g fibre

tip Any leftover stock can be frozen for up to 3 months; use in chowders, seafood soups, stews and curries.

CAULIFLOWER RICE & GINGER CHICKEN CONGEE

PREP + COOK TIME 1 HOUR 20 MINUTES **SERVES** 4

4CM (1½-INCH) PIECE FRESH GINGER (20G), SLICED THINLY

2 CHICKEN BREAST FILLETS (400G)

1 CUP (30G) DRIED SHIITAKE MUSHROOMS

2 TEASPOONS BONITO FLAKES (SEE TIPS)

1.5 LITRES (6 CUPS) SALT-REDUCED CHICKEN STOCK

½ CUP (125ML) LIGHT SOY SAUCE

1 CUP (250ML) CHINESE COOKING WINE (SHAO HSING)

1 TABLESPOON PEANUT OIL

3 TEASPOONS GRATED FRESH GINGER

6 CLOVES GARLIC, CHOPPED FINELY

4 GREEN ONIONS (SCALLIONS), SLICED THINLY, GREEN AND WHITE PARTS SEPERATED

1KG (2 POUNDS) CAULIFLOWER, BROKEN INTO FLORETS

¼ CUP (20G) QUINOA FLAKES

½ CUP LOOSELY PACKED FRESH CORIANDER (CILANTRO) LEAVES

1 TABLESPOON ASIAN CHILLI OIL

1 TABLESPOON SESAME OIL

1 Place sliced ginger in a medium saucepan with chicken, shiitake mushrooms, bonito flakes, stock, soy sauce and wine; bring to the boil. Cover with a tight-fitting lid; simmer over low heat for 20 minutes.

2 Remove chicken from stock mixture. Strain stock mixture into a heatproof large jug or bowl; reserve mushrooms. Discard remaining solids. When cool enough to handle, shred chicken; slice mushrooms, keeping some whole.

3 Meanwhile, heat oil in a large saucepan over medium heat. Cook grated ginger, garlic and the white part of the green onions for 3 minutes or until softened.

4 Process cauliflower florets in batches using the pulse button 8-10 times or until it resembles grains of rice. Add cauliflower to the pan; cook, stirring, for 2 minutes.

5 Add the reserved stock, mushrooms and the quinoa flakes; bring to the boil. Reduce heat to medium; simmer, stirring occasionally, for 30 minutes. Add the shredded chicken to warm through. Season to taste.

6 Divide congee between bowls; top with remaining sliced green onion and the coriander. Serve immediately drizzled with chilli oil and sesame oil.

nutritional count per serving 18g total fat (3g saturated fat); 1587kJ (379 cal); 25g carbohydrate; 30g protein; 7g fibre

tips Dried bonito flakes are available from Asian food stores. Shao hsing (also known as shaoxing), Chinese cooking wine, is available from some supermarkets and Asian food stores. You can omit the chilli oil, if you like.

PEPITA & SUNFLOWER SEED RICE WITH POACHED TURKEY

PREP + COOK TIME 45 MINUTES (+ STANDING) **SERVES** 4

500G (1 POUND) TURKEY BREASTS, HALVED LENGTHWAYS

½ CUP (100G) PEPITAS (PUMPKIN SEED KERNELS)

1 CUP (150G) SUNFLOWER SEEDS

400G (12½ OUNCES) BROCCOLI

¼ CUP (60ML) EXTRA VIRGIN OLIVE OIL

1 MEDIUM RED ONION (170G), CHOPPED FINELY

3 CLOVES GARLIC, CRUSHED

3 FRESH THYME SPRIGS

2 TEASPOONS FINELY GRATED LEMON RIND

¼ CUP (60ML) FRESH LEMON JUICE

½ CUP LOOSELY PACKED FRESH FLAT-LEAF PARSLEY LEAVES

⅓ CUP LOOSELY PACKED FRESH MINT LEAVES

50G (1½ OUNCES) SOFT GOAT'S CHEESE, CRUMBLED

1 Preheat oven to 180°C/350°F.

2 Bring a large saucepan of salted water to the boil; add turkey. Return to the boil; turn off heat. Cover, stand for 20 minutes or until just cooked through. Remove turkey from water. When cool enough to handle, shred coarsely.

3 Meanwhile, spread pepitas and sunflower seeds on an oven tray. Roast for 10 minutes; cool.

4 Remove the broccoli florets from the stem; reserve stems for another use (see tips). Process the florets in a food processor.

5 Heat 2 tablespoons of the oil in a large deep-sided frying pan over medium heat. Cook onion, garlic and thyme, stirring occasionally, for 5 minutes or until onion is soft. Add broccoli; cook, stirring, for 4 minutes or until broccoli is tender.

6 Transfer broccoli mixture to a large bowl; add rind, juice, toasted seeds, parsley, half the mint and the shredded turkey. Season to taste.

7 Transfer to a serving platter; drizzle with remaining oil. Top with goat's cheese and remaining mint leaves.

nutritional count per serving 54g total fat (9g saturated fat); 3035kJ (725 cal); 4g carbohydrate; 51g protein; 10g fibre

tips Broccoli stems can be trimmed and sliced; use them in stir-fries or roast with a little oil and garlic. You can make this salad with chicken breast fillets, or use a barbecued cooked chicken, if you like.

PIZZAS
&TARTS

SMOKED SALMON & AVOCADO KALE PIZZA

PREP + COOK TIME 1 HOUR 5 MINUTES **SERVES** 4

400G (12½ OUNCES) KALE, TRIMMED, LEAVES ONLY, CHOPPED COARSELY

3 CUPS (300G) GRATED MOZZARELLA

4 EGGS

1⅓ CUPS (100G) PANKO (JAPANESE) BREADCRUMBS

1 SMALL RED ONION (100G), SLICED THINLY

200G (6½ OUNCES) SLICED SMOKED SALMON

1 MEDIUM AVOCADO (250G), SLICED

2 CUPS (35G) BABY ROCKET LEAVES

1 MEDIUM LEMON (140G), CUT INTO 4 WEDGES

DILL & HORSERADISH CREAM CHEESE

185G (6 OUNCES) BLOCK LIGHT CREAM CHEESE, SOFTENED

¼ CUP CHOPPED FRESH DILL

2 TABLESPOONS HORSERADISH CREAM

2 TEASPOONS FINELY GRATED LEMON RIND

1 Preheat oven to 240°C/475°F. Line two large oven trays with baking paper.

2 Process kale, in two batches, until finely chopped. Return kale to processor; add 2 cups of the mozzarella, the eggs and breadcrumbs. Process until a sticky dough forms. Divide dough in half. Spread dough over trays to make two 22cm x 32cm (8¾-inch x 12¾-inch) rectangles.

3 Bake bases for 20 minutes. Turn bases over and bake for a further 5 minutes or until edges are browned.

4 Meanwhile, make dill and horseradish cream cheese.

5 Spread cream cheese mixture over bases. Top with onion and remaining mozzarella. Bake for 10 minutes or until cheese is melted and golden.

6 Top pizzas with smoked salmon, avocado and rocket. Serve with lemon wedges.

dill & horseradish cream cheese Combine all ingredients in a medium bowl. (Makes 1¼ cups)

nutritional count per serving 48g total fat (23g saturated fat); 3062kJ (732 cal); 24g carbohydrate; 45g protein; 7g fibre

tips You will need one bunch of kale for this recipe. Use the kale stalks in soups, stocks or stews. An off-set or cranked spatula is useful to spread the mixture over the trays.

do-ahead Cream cheese mixture can be made a day ahead. Stand at room temperature for 20 minutes and beat lightly until spreadable before using. Bases can be made, to the end of step 3, several hours ahead.

PROSCIUTTO &
ROCKET SOCCA PIZZAS

PREP + COOK TIME 1 HOUR (+ STANDING) **MAKES** 4

2 CUPS (300G) CHICKPEA FLOUR (BESAN)

1 TEASPOON GARLIC POWDER

2⅓ CUPS (580ML) WATER

¼ CUP (60ML) EXTRA VIRGIN OLIVE OIL

3 HEIRLOOM TOMATOES (420G)

1 SMALL CLOVE GARLIC, CRUSHED

¼ CUP LOOSELY PACKED FRESH BASIL LEAVES

2 BUFFALO MOZZARELLA (260G), SLICED

200G (6½ OUNCES) SHAVED PROSCIUTTO, TORN COARSELY

2 CUPS (35G) BABY ROCKET LEAVES

⅓ CUP (25G) FLAKED PARMESAN

2 TEASPOONS EXTRA VIRGIN OLIVE OIL, EXTRA

1 Combine chickpea flour and garlic powder in a large jug; season. Whisk in the water and oil; stand for 30 minutes.
2 Meanwhile, blend or process one chopped tomato with garlic and basil until smooth; season.
3 Preheat oven to 240°C/475°F. Line two large oven trays with baking paper.
4 Heat a greased 27cm (10¾-inch) wide, 20cm (8-inch) base frying pan over medium heat. Add ¼ of the chickpea mixture to the pan. Cook, for 5 minutes or until cooked through and base is golden and crisp. Slide base out of pan on to tray, browned side down. Repeat to make 4 bases in total.
5 Spread bases with the tomato mixture. Top with mozzarella. Slice remaining tomatoes; place over mozzarella.
6 Bake pizzas for 15 minutes or until golden and crisp. Top with prosciutto, rocket and parmesan; drizzle with extra oil.

nutritional count per pizza 51g total fat (19g saturated fat); 3461kJ (827 cal); 41g carbohydrate; 46g protein; 10g fibre
tips Chickpea flour is available from some supermarkets and health food stores. Buffalo mozzarella is available from some large supermarkets or delis. You can use large bocconcini instead. Use whatever pizza toppings that are your favourite. You can use ripe truss tomatoes in place of heirloom.
do-ahead This recipe can be made, to the end of step 4, several hours ahead. Keep bases in an airtight container and tomato mixture in the fridge.

PANCETTA & FIG SWEET POTATO PIZZAS

PREP + COOK TIME 55 MINUTES **SERVES** 4 (MAKES 8)

2 LARGE ORANGE SWEET POTATOES (1KG)

2 TABLESPOONS EXTRA VIRGIN OLIVE OIL

100G (3 OUNCES) PANCETTA, TORN COARSELY

60G (2 OUNCES) GORGONZOLA, CRUMBLED

8 DRIED FIGS (120G)

1⅓ CUPS (135G) GRATED MOZZARELLA

⅔ CUP LOOSELY PACKED FRESH BASIL LEAVES

1 Preheat oven to 220°C/425°F. Line two large oven trays with baking paper.

2 Cut each sweet potato lengthways into four 1cm (½-inch) thick slices. Place sweet potato on trays, drizzle with oil; season. Roast for 25 minutes. Turn sweet potato over. Top with pancetta and gorgonzola. Cut figs horizontally into three slices. Divide fig and mozzarella between pizzas.

3 Roast pizzas for a further 10 minutes or until golden. Sprinkle with basil and extra gorgonzola, if you like.

nutritional count per serving 15g total fat (6g saturated fat); 1175kJ (281 cal); 25g carbohydrate; 10g protein; 6g fibre

tips If you choose a short, wide sweet potato, it will be easier to cut. Leave the skin on when slicing the sweet potato. Gorgonzola is an Italian blue cheese with a soft crumbly texture; you can use your favourite soft cheese, if you prefer. You could use fresh figs when they are in season.

serving suggestion Serve with a mixed leaf salad.

HONEY-ROASTED EGGPLANT TART

PREP + COOK TIME 55 MINUTES (+ STANDING & COOLING) **SERVES** 6

½ CUP (85G) POLENTA (CORNMEAL) (SEE TIP)

1½ CUPS (180G) ALMOND MEAL

1 TABLESPOON CUMIN SEEDS

1 TEASPOON SEA SALT FLAKES

80G (2½ OUNCES) COLD BUTTER, CHOPPED

1 TABLESPOON ICED WATER

1 LARGE EGGPLANT (500G), CUT INTO
3CM (1¼-INCH) PIECES

2 TABLESPOONS EXTRA VIRGIN OLIVE OIL

1 TABLESPOON HONEY

1 CUP (280G) GREEK-STYLE YOGHURT

¼ CUP (60ML) TAHINI

1 FRESH LONG RED CHILLI, CHOPPED FINELY

1 CLOVE GARLIC, CRUSHED

2 TEASPOONS FRESH LEMON JUICE

2 TABLESPOONS POMEGRANATE SEEDS

½ CUP LOOSELY PACKED FRESH CORIANDER
(CILANTRO) LEAVES

1 Preheat oven to 200°C/400°F. Grease an 11.5cm x 35cm (4¾-inch x 14-inch) fluted rectangular tart tin. Line an oven tray with baking paper.

2 Process polenta, almond meal, cumin seeds and salt until combined. Add butter; pulse until resembles crumbs. Add water a little at a time; pulse until mixture holds together when pinched. Press mixture evenly over base and sides of tin, using the back of a wet spoon. Place tin on an oven tray.

3 Combine eggplant, oil and honey; place on tray, season. Bake eggplant mixture and tart case, stirring eggplant once, for 30 minutes or until eggplant is golden and tart case is firm and lightly golden. Leave tart in tin for 15 minutes before transferring to a wire rack to cool.

4 Meanwhile, combine yoghurt, tahini, chilli, garlic and juice in a medium bowl; season to taste. Spread yoghurt mixture over base of tart case. Top with eggplant mixture, pomegranate seeds and coriander.

nutritional count per serving 44g total fat (11g saturated fat); 2284kJ (546 cal); 22g carbohydrate; 14g protein; 7g fibre

tip For best results, use a fine polenta for this recipe, as they vary in texture from fine to coarse, depending on the brand.

do-ahead You can make the tart case, eggplant mixture and tahini yoghurt several hours ahead. Assemble the tart just before serving.

SMOKY HAM & BROCCOLINI PIZZAS

PREP + COOK TIME 1 HOUR (+ STANDING) **SERVES** 4 (MAKES 2)

You will need to start this recipe a day ahead.

1½ CUPS (300G) WHITE QUINOA

1 TEASPOON BAKING POWDER

1 TEASPOON SEA SALT FLAKES

½ CUP (125ML) WATER

2 TABLESPOONS EXTRA VIRGIN OLIVE OIL

½ CUP (125ML) BOTTLED TOMATO PASSATA

½ TEASPOON SMOKED PAPRIKA

75G (2½ OUNCES) SMOKED LEG HAM, TORN COARSELY

¾ CUP (75G) GRATED MOZZARELLA

¾ CUP (90G) GRATED SMOKED CHEDDAR

70G (2½ OUNCES) BROCCOLINI, HALVED LENGTHWAYS

1 FRESH LONG RED CHILLI, CHOPPED

¼ CUP (30G) SEEDED BLACK OLIVES, SLICED

1 Place quinoa in a large bowl; cover with cold water. Stand for at least 8 hours or overnight. Drain; rinse well.

2 Preheat oven to 240°C/475°F. Line two large oven trays with baking paper.

3 Place quinoa, baking powder, salt, water and oil in a high-powered blender; blend until smooth.

4 Heat a greased 30cm (12-inch) wide, 25cm (10-inch) base frying pan over medium heat. Cook half quinoa mixture in pan for 5 minutes or until golden and crisp. Turn base-side-up onto one tray. Repeat with remaining mixture. Bake bases for 15 minutes or until crisp, swapping trays halfway through cooking time.

5 Combine passata and paprika in a small bowl; spread over bases. Top with ham, mozzarella, cheddar, broccolini, chilli and olives.

6 Bake pizzas for 10 minutes or until cheeses are melted and golden. Top with baby kale or rocket, if you like.

nutritional count per serving 28g total fat (10g saturated fat); 2310kJ (552 cal); 47g carbohydrate; 24g protein; 7g fibre

tip You can add your favourite pizza toppings in step 5.

do-ahead Recipe can be made, to the end of step 4, several hours ahead.

SPRING VEGETABLE & LABNEH TARTS

PREP + COOK TIME 1 HOUR 5 MINUTES (+ REFRIGERATION & COOLING) **MAKES** 4

¾ CUP (150G) TRI-COLOURED QUINOA

1½ CUPS (375ML) WATER

¼ CUP (40G) SUNFLOWER SEEDS

1 CUP (80G) FINELY GRATED PARMESAN

1 EGG

1 SMALL ZUCCHINI (90G)

1 MEDIUM LEMON (140G), SLICED THINLY

⅓ CUP (40G) FROZEN PEAS

80G (2½ OUNCES) ASPARAGUS

¼ CUP LOOSELY PACKED FRESH MINT LEAVES

HERB & GARLIC LABNEH

250G (8 OUNCES) LABNEH (SEE TIPS)

1 CLOVE GARLIC, CRUSHED

2 TABLESPOONS FINELY CHOPPED
FRESH MINT LEAVES

1 TABLESPOON CHOPPED FRESH CHIVES

1 Place quinoa and the water in a medium saucepan; bring to the boil. Reduce heat; cook, covered, for 15 minutes or until tender. Drain; cool.

2 Grease four 12cm (4¾-inch) (inside top measurement) round loose-based tart tins well.

3 Process quinoa, sunflower seeds and ¾ cup of the parmesan until quinoa is finely chopped. Add egg and season with salt; process until mixture forms a coarse dough. Press mixture evenly over base and sides of tins using the back of a wet spoon. Refrigerate for 30 minutes or until firm.

4 Meanwhile, preheat oven to 200°C/400°F. Place an oven tray in oven to heat. Sprinkle tart shells with remaining parmesan. Place on hot tray. Bake for 35 minutes or until golden and crisp. Remove tart shells from tins; transfer to a wire rack.

5 Using a vegetable peeler or mandoline, peel zucchini into long thin ribbons. Cook zucchini first, then lemon slices, on a heated lightly oiled grill pan (or barbecue) for 1 minute each side or until browned. Pour boiling water over peas in a small heatproof bowl; stand for 1 minute, drain.

6 Make herb and garlic labneh.

7 Using a vegetable peeler or mandoline, peel asparagus into long thin ribbons. Fill the cooled tarts with the labneh. Top with the zucchini, asparagus, peas, lemon and mint.

herb & garlic labneh Combine all ingredients in a medium bowl; season to taste.

nutritional count per tart 20g total fat (7g saturated fat); 1629kJ (389 cal); 27g carbohydrate; 22g protein; 6g fibre

tips Labneh is a thick drained yoghurt cheese, available from some large supermarkets and delis. It can be expensive, but it's very easy to make at home. To make your own, line a medium sieve with muslin. Place sieve over a jug or bowl. Spoon 500g (1 pound) Greek-style yoghurt into sieve. Cover, refrigerate overnight or for 24 hours. This will make a little more than you need for this recipe. Leftover plain labneh can be served with grilled lamb or served spread on toasted fruit bread, with fruit or sweetened and served with cake or dessert.

do-ahead You can make the herb and garlic labneh and tart shells 6 hours ahead; fill tarts just before serving.

FREE-FORM BEETROOT, RICOTTA CREAM & HAZELNUT TART

PREP + COOK TIME 1 HOUR 10 MINUTES **SERVES** 6

3 MEDIUM BEETROOT (BEETS) (525G), PEELED, CUT INTO 1CM (½-INCH) SLICES

1 LARGE RED ONION (300G), QUARTERED

1½ TABLESPOONS FRESH THYME LEAVES

¼ CUP (60ML) EXTRA VIRGIN OLIVE OIL

2 TABLESPOONS RED WINE VINEGAR

700G (1½ POUNDS) ORANGE SWEET POTATOES, CHOPPED COARSELY

1½ CUPS (150G) HAZELNUT MEAL

1 EGG, BEATEN LIGHTLY

½ CUP (65G) GRATED GRUYÈRE CHEESE

⅓ CUP (45G) SKINLESS ROASTED HAZELNUTS, CHOPPED COARSELY

40G (1½ OUNCES) BABY SPINACH LEAVES

RICOTTA CREAM

1½ CUPS (360G) FRESH RICOTTA

2 TEASPOONS FINELY GRATED LEMON RIND

1 TABLESPOON FRESH LEMON JUICE

2 CLOVES GARLIC, CRUSHED

1 Preheat oven to 200°C/400°F. Line two large oven trays with baking paper.

2 Place beetroot and onion on one tray. Sprinkle vegetables with 1 tablespoon of the thyme and drizzle with 1 tablespoon each of the oil and the vinegar; season. Roast for 40 minutes or until tender.

3 Meanwhile, boil or steam sweet potato for 10 minutes or until soft; drain.

4 Place the sweet potato in a large bowl; mash until smooth. Stir in the hazelnut meal, egg and cheese; season to taste. Spread mixture over remaining tray into a 28cm x 36cm (11¼-inch x 14½-inch) rectangle, about 1cm (½-inch) thick. Bake for 30 minutes or until set and the edges are golden.

5 Meanwhile, make ricotta cream.

6 Spread ricotta cream over base. Top with beetroot, onion, remaining thyme leaves, the chopped hazelnuts and spinach. Drizzle with remaining oil and vinegar.

ricotta cream Whisk all ingredients in a large bowl until smooth and well combined; season to taste.

nutritional count per serving 39.4g total fat (8.3g saturated fat); 2385kJ (570 cal); 28.4g carbohydrate; 20.2g protein; 10.3g fibre

tips You can use cottage cheese instead of ricotta. This tart is best served warm or at room temperature.

do-ahead The sweet potato tart base can be made several hours ahead.

BEETROOT RÖSTI TARTS WITH BRESAOLA & HORSERADISH CREAM

PREP + COOK TIME 55 MINUTES (+ COOLING) **MAKES** 6

3 LARGE BEETROOT (BEETS) (600G), PEELED, GRATED COARSELY

¼ CUP (40G) WHOLEMEAL PLAIN (ALL-PURPOSE) FLOUR

2 EGGS, BEATEN LIGHTLY

2 CUPS (80G) FIRMLY PACKED TRIMMED WATERCRESS

150G (4½ OUNCES) BRESAOLA

1½ TABLESPOONS BABY CAPERS

HORSERADISH CRUMBLE

1½ TABLESPOONS HORSERADISH CREAM

⅓ CUP (40G) ALMOND MEAL

HORSERADISH CREAM

200G (6½ OUNCES) CRÈME FRAÎCHE

¼ CUP (70G) HORSERADISH CREAM

2 TABLESPOONS FRESH LEMON JUICE

1 TEASPOON WORCESTERSHIRE SAUCE

1 Preheat oven to 180°C/350°F. Wrap beetroot in a clean tea towel or muslin. Squeeze out excess liquid; transfer to a large bowl. Add flour and egg, season; mix well. Press mixture into six greased 12cm (4¾-inch) (inside top measurement) shallow tart tins.

2 Bake tart cases for 30 minutes or until crisp; cool in tins.

3 Meanwhile, make horseradish crumble and horseradish cream.

4 Divide horseradish cream among tart cases. Top with watercress, bresaola, capers and horseradish crumble.

horseradish crumble Rub horseradish cream into almond meal in a small bowl. Sprinkle mixture over a baking-paper-lined oven tray. Bake in oven with tart cases, on a seperate shelf, for 5 minutes. Using a spatula or fork, break up gently. Bake for a further 2 minutes or until golden and crisp.

horseradish cream Combine all ingredients in a small bowl; season to taste.

nutritional count per tart 21g total fat (10g saturated fat); 1355kJ (324 cal); 16g carbohydrate; 16g protein; 5g fibre

tip Leftover horseradish cream can be refrigerated for up to 2 days. Serve with roast or grilled beef or grilled salmon.

do-ahead You can make the recipe, to the end of step 3, several hours ahead. Assemble just before serving.

CAULIFLOWER TORTILLAS
WITH PULLED PORK

PREP + COOK TIME 3 HOURS 20 MINUTES **SERVES** 6 (MAKES 18)

1 TABLESPOON EXTRA VIRGIN OLIVE OIL

1 MEDIUM ONION (150G), CHOPPED

1 TEASPOON DRIED OREGANO

2 BAY LEAVES

4 CLOVES GARLIC, CRUSHED

¼ CUP (70G) TOMATO PASTE

1.2KG (2½-POUND) BONELESS PORK SHOULDER, RIND REMOVED

1 FRESH THYME SPRIG

400G (12½ OUNCES) CANNED DICED TOMATOES

3 DRAINED CHIPOTLE CHILLIES (45G), CHOPPED FINELY (SEE TIP)

1 CUP (250ML) WATER

1 MEDIUM AVOCADO (250G), SLICED

4 SMALL RED RADISH (60G), SLICED THINLY

1 SMALL RED ONION (100G), SLICED THINLY

200G (6½ OUNCES) GRAPE TOMATOES, HALVED

1 CUP LOOSELY PACKED FRESH CORIANDER (CILANTRO) LEAVES

½ CUP (120G) SOUR CREAM

CAULIFLOWER TORTILLAS

2KG (4 POUNDS) CHOPPED CAULIFLOWER

4 EGGS, BEATEN LIGHTLY

1 Heat oil in a large saucepan over medium heat. Cook onion, oregano, bay leaves and garlic, stirring, for 5 minutes or until soft. Stir in paste; cook, stirring, for 1 minute. Add pork, thyme, tomatoes, half the chilli and the water; bring to the boil. Reduce heat to low; simmer, covered, for 2½ hours or until pork is starting to fall apart, turning pork over in sauce occasionally. Discard bay leaves.

2 Meanwhile, make cauliflower tortillas.

3 Transfer pork to a large bowl; shred with two forks, discarding any large pieces of fat or gristle. Season to taste. Stir half the sauce back into the pork.

4 Serve pork in cauliflower tortillas topped with remaining sauce, avocado, radish, red onion, grape tomatoes and coriander. Dollop with combined sour cream and remaining chilli.

cauliflower tortillas Preheat oven to 200°C/400°F. Process cauliflower using pulse button until pieces are finely chopped. Steam or microwave cauliflower, in two batches, for 3 minutes or until tender. Stand until cool enough to handle. Place cauliflower in a clean tea towel; squeeze out as much water as possible. This is important for dry tortillas. Transfer cauliflower to a large bowl. Stir in egg; season. Divide mixture in 18 equal portions. Line two oven trays with baking paper. Mark two 13cm (5¼-inch) rounds on paper; turn paper over. Spread cauliflower portions in rounds on trays; bake for 8 minutes. Carefully turn tortillas over using a spatula; bake for a further 8 minutes or until browned around the edges. Repeat with remaining cauliflower mixture to make 18 tortillas in total.

nutritional count per serving 28g total fat (10g saturated fat); 2197kJ (525 cal); 12g carbohydrate; 52g protein; 10g fibre

tip Chipotle chilli in adobo sauce is available in cans from some delis and large supermarkets.

do-ahead You can cook pulled pork up to a day ahead; reheat in the pan juices before serving. Cauliflower tortillas can be made several hours ahead. Layer between pieces of baking paper; cover and refrigerate for up to 3 hours. Reheat wrapped in foil in a 180°C/350°F oven for 10 minutes or until heated through.

SPICY LAMB & SILVER BEET ZUCCHINI PIZZAS

PREP + COOK TIME 55 MINUTES (+ STANDING) **SERVES** 2

3 MEDIUM ZUCCHINI (360G), GRATED COARSELY

½ CUP (40G) FINELY GRATED PARMESAN

½ CUP (75G) PLAIN (ALL-PURPOSE) FLOUR

2 EGGS, BEATEN LIGHTLY

3 MEDIUM LEAVES SILVER BEET (SWISS CHARD) (180G)

100G (3 OUNCES) MINCED (GROUND) LAMB, CRUMBLED

½ CUP (120G) REDUCED-FAT RICOTTA

1 CUP (100G) GRATED MOZZARELLA

2 TABLESPOONS FRESH OREGANO LEAVES

HARISSA PASSATA

¼ CUP (60ML) BOTTLED TOMATO PASSATA

1 TEASPOON HARISSA PASTE

1 CLOVE GARLIC, CRUSHED

1 Preheat oven to 240°C/475°F. Line two large oven trays with baking paper. Mark 25cm (10-inch) rounds on paper; turn paper over.

2 Place zucchini in a clean tea towel; squeeze out as much liquid as possible. Place zucchini in a large bowl. Stir in the parmesan, flour and egg until combined; season. Spread zucchini mixture over rounds on trays.

3 Bake zucchini bases for 20 minutes. Turn over; bake for a further 5 minutes or until crisp and golden.

4 Meanwhile, make harissa passata.

5 Remove stalks from silver beet. Slice leaves. Pour boiling water over silver beet in a medium heatproof bowl; stand for 20 seconds, drain well, pat dry. Spread bases with harissa passata. Top with silver beet, lamb, ricotta and mozzarella.

6 Bake pizzas for 10 minutes or until cheese is melted and golden. Serve sprinkled with oregano leaves.

harissa passata Combine all ingredients in a small bowl; season to taste.

nutritional count per serving 29g total fat (15g saturated fat); 2600kJ (621 cal); 36g carbohydrate; 48g protein; 7g fibre

serving suggestion Serve with lemon wedges.

ROAST PUMPKIN WITH WILD MUSHROOMS & PECORINO

PREP + COOK TIME 55 MINUTES **SERVES** 2

1KG (2 POUNDS) BUTTERNUT PUMPKIN (SEE TIPS)

1 TEASPOON FINELY GRATED LEMON RIND

OLIVE OIL COOKING SPRAY

100G (3 OUNCES) SHIITAKE MUSHROOMS, SLICED

100G (3 OUNCES) SWISS BROWN MUSHROOMS, SLICED

100G (3 OUNCES) KING BROWN MUSHROOMS, SLICED

100G (3 OUNCES) BUTTON MUSHROOMS, SLICED

2 CLOVES GARLIC, CHOPPED FINELY

70G (2½ OUNCES) SHAVED PECORINO CHEESE

4 FRESH THYME SPRIGS

PORCINI BUTTER

10G (½ OUNCE) DRIED PORCINI MUSHROOMS

80G (2½ OUNCES) BUTTER, SOFTENED

1 Preheat oven to 200°C/400°F. Line an oven tray with baking paper.

2 Leaving skin on, slice the long end of the pumpkin into four rounds, about 3cm (1¼-inch) thick. Place rounds on tray; sprinkle with lemon rind, spray with oil. Roast pumpkin for 40 minutes or until golden and cooked through.

3 Make porcini butter.

4 Heat half the porcini butter in a large frying pan over medium heat. Cook mushrooms, stirring occasionally, for 10 minutes or until golden brown. Add garlic; cook, stirring, for 1 minute or until fragrant. Season to taste.

5 Warm remaining porcini butter in a small saucepan.

6 Divide pumpkin rounds between two serving plates. Top with mushroom mixture, pecorino and sprinkle with thyme. Drizzle with porcini butter; season to taste. Serve with mixed salad leaves, if you like.

porcini butter Process porcini in a high-powered blender or spice grinder to a fine powder. Cook 2 teaspoons of the powder with the butter in a small saucepan over medium heat until melted; simmer for 2 minutes.

nutritional count per serving 23.5g total fat (14g saturated fat); 1378kJ (329 cal); 14.2g carbohydrate; 11.8g protein; 5.5g fibre

tips You will need the long end, without the seeds, of the butternut pumpkin. Use a selection of seasonally available mushrooms for the topping.

VEGIE RÖSTI WITH SMOKED SALMON & WATERCRESS

PREP + COOK TIME 40 MINUTES **MAKES** 4

1 MEDIUM ZUCCHINI (120G)

1 LARGE CARROT (180G)

1 MEDIUM LEEK (350G), CUT INTO MATCHSTICKS

1 LARGE RED CAPSICUM (BELL PEPPER) (350G), SLICED THINLY

1 CUP (240G) RICOTTA

½ CUP (50G) GRATED MOZZARELLA

1 EGG, BEATEN LIGHTLY

50G (1½ OUNCES) WATERCRESS SPRIGS

1 TEASPOON RED WINE VINEGAR

1 TABLESPOON EXTRA VIRGIN OLIVE OIL

200G (6½ OUNCES) SLICED SMOKED SALMON

1 Preheat oven to 180°C/350°F. Line an oven tray with baking paper.

2 Using a vegetable peeler, peel zucchini and carrot into long thin ribbons. Combine zucchini and carrot with leek, capsicum, ricotta, mozzarella and egg in a large bowl; season well.

3 Press a quarter of the vegie mixture into a 10cm (4-inch) round cutter on the tray. Remove cutter; repeat with remaining vegie mixture to make 4 rounds in total. Bake for 25 minutes or until browned lightly and crisp.

4 Meanwhile, combine watercress, vinegar and oil in a medium bowl; season to taste.

5 Transfer vegie rösti to a platter; top evenly with smoked salmon and watercress mixture. Season to taste.

nutritional count per pizza 19g total fat (7g saturated fat); 1351kJ (323 cal); 9g carbohydrate; 25g protein; 5g fibre

tips The rösti could also be topped with crisp prosciutto, goat's curd or olive tapenade. Garnish with chopped chives, if you like.

quinoa pizza base

polenta crust

socca pizza base

sweet potato crust

zucchini pizza base

quinoa tart shells

Bases & Cases

Finish these bases and cases with your favourite toppings; fresh greens, sautéed vegetables or grilled meat.

SWEET POTATO CRUST

prep + cook time 50 minutes **serves** 6

Preheat oven to 200°C/400°F. Line a large oven tray with baking paper. Boil or steam 700g (1½lbs) coarsely chopped orange sweet potatoes for 10 minutes or until soft; drain. Place sweet potato in a large bowl; mash until smooth. Stir in 1½ cups (150g) hazelnut meal, 1 lightly beaten egg and ½ cup (65g) grated gruyère cheese; season to taste. Spread mixture over tray into a 28cm x 36cm (11¼in x 14½in) rectangle, about 1cm (½-in) thick. Bake base for 30 minutes or until set and the edges are golden.

do-ahead The sweet potato base can be made several hours ahead.

QUINOA PIZZA BASE

prep + cook time 40 minutes (+ standing) **serves** 4 (makes 2)

You will need to start this recipe a day ahead.

Place 1½ cups (300g) white quinoa in a large bowl; cover with cold water. Stand for at least 8 hours or overnight. Drain; rinse well. Preheat oven to 240°C/475°F. Line two large oven trays with baking paper. Place quinoa, 1 teaspoon baking powder, 1 teaspoon sea salt flakes, ½ cup (125ml) water and 2 tablespoons extra virgin olive oil in a high-speed blender; blend until smooth. Heat a greased 30cm (12-in) wide, 25cm (10-in) base frying pan over medium heat. Cook half quinoa mixture in pan for 5 minutes or until golden and crisp. Turn base-side-up onto tray. Repeat with remaining mixture. Bake bases for 15 minutes or until crisp, swapping trays halfway through cooking time.

do-ahead Recipe can be made several hours ahead. Store cooled bases in an airtight container.

SOCCA PIZZA BASE

prep + cook time 30 minutes (+ standing) **makes** 4

Preheat oven to 240°C/475°F. Line two large oven trays with baking paper. Combine 2 cups (300g) chickpea flour (besan) and 1 teaspoon garlic powder in a large jug; season. Whisk in 2⅓ cups (580ml) water and ¼ cup (60ml) extra virgin olive oil; stand for 30 minutes. Heat a greased 27cm (10¾-in) wide, 20cm (8-in) base frying pan over medium heat. Add ¼ of the chickpea mixture to the pan. Cook, for 5 minutes or until cooked through and base is golden and crisp. Slide base out of pan on to tray, browned side down. Repeat to make 4 bases in total.

tip Chickpea flour is available from some supermarkets and health food stores.

do-ahead Recipe can be made several hours ahead. Keep bases in an airtight container.

POLENTA CRUST

prep + cook time 45 minutes (+ standing & cooling) **serves** 6

Preheat oven to 200°C/400°F. Grease an 11cm x 35cm (4½-in x 14-in) fluted rectangular tart tin. Line an oven tray with baking paper. Process ½ cup (85g) polenta (cornmeal), 1½ cups (180g) almond meal, 1 tablespoon cumin seeds and 1 teaspoon sea salt flakes until combined. Add 80g (2½oz) cold butter, chopped; pulse until resembles crumbs. Add enough of 1 tablespoon iced water to make ingredients hold together when pinched. Press mixture evenly over base and sides of tin using back of a wet spoon. Place tin on an oven tray. Bake for 30 minutes or until tart case is firm and lightly golden. Stand 15 minutes before transferring to a wire rack to cool.

tip Use a fine polenta for this recipe as they vary from fine to coarse depending on the brand.

do-ahead You can make the tart case several hours ahead.

QUINOA TART SHELLS

prep + cook time 1 hour (+ cooling & refrigeration) **makes** 4

Place ¾ cup (150g) tri-coloured quinoa and 1½ cups (375ml) water in a medium saucepan; bring to the boil. Reduce heat; cook, covered, for 15 minutes or until tender. Drain; cool. Grease four 12.5cm (5-in) round loose-based tart tins well. Process quinoa, ¼ cup (40g) sunflower seeds and ¾ cup (60g) finely grated parmesan until quinoa is finely chopped. Add 1 egg; season with salt. Process until mixture forms a coarse dough. Press mixture over base and side of tins using back of a wet spoon. Refrigerate 30 minutes until firm. Preheat oven to 200°C/400°F. Place oven tray in oven to heat. Sprinkle tart shells with ¼ cup (20g) finely grated parmesan. Place on hot tray. Bake tart shells for 35 minutes or until golden and crisp. Turn top-side-up onto a wire rack to cool.

ZUCCHINI PIZZA BASE

prep + cook time 40 minutes (+ standing) **serves** 2

Preheat oven to 240°C/475°F. Line two large oven trays with baking paper. Mark 25cm (10-in) rounds on paper; turn paper over. Place 3 coarsely grated medium zucchini (360g) in a clean tea towel; squeeze out as much liquid as possible. Place zucchini in a large bowl. Stir in ½ cup (40g) finely grated parmesan, ½ cup (75g) plain (all-purpose) flour and 2 lightly beaten eggs until combined; season. Spread zucchini mixture over rounds on trays. Bake zucchini bases for 20 minutes. Turn over; bake for a further 5 minutes or until crisp and golden.

PRAWN & VEGETABLE JAPANESE HASH BROWNS

PREP + COOK TIME 35 MINUTES **SERVES** 4 (MAKES 12)

12 COOKED MEDIUM KING PRAWNS (SHRIMP) (540G)

2 GREEN ONIONS (SCALLIONS)

4 EGGS

¼ CUP (30G) ALMOND MEAL

250G (8 OUNCES) BUTTERNUT PUMPKIN, GRATED COARSELY

1 MEDIUM ORANGE SWEET POTATO (400G), GRATED COARSELY

1½ CUPS (120G) SHREDDED CABBAGE

¼ CUP (60ML) RICE BRAN OIL

¼ CUP (75G) JAPANESE MAYONNAISE

½ TEASPOON WHITE SESAME SEEDS, TOASTED

½ TEASPOON BLACK SESAME SEEDS, TOASTED

1 TABLESPOON PICKLED GINGER

1 Shell and devein prawns, leaving tails intact.

2 Finely chop one green onion; thinly slice remaining onion.

3 Whisk eggs, almond meal and the finely chopped onion in a large bowl until combined. Stir in pumpkin, sweet potato and 1 cup of the cabbage; season to taste.

4 Heat oil in a large frying pan over medium heat. Working in batches, spoon ¼ cup measures of mixture into pan; spread slightly. Cook for 2 minutes each side or until golden and cooked through. You will need a total of 12 hash browns.

5 Top hash browns with prawns, remaining cabbage and green onion. Drizzle with mayonnaise and sprinkle with combined seeds. Serve with pickled ginger.

nutritional count per serving 39g total fat (7g saturated fat); 2284kJ (546 cal); 19g carbohydrate; 26g protein; 5g fibre

tips You can buy japanese mayonnaise from some supermarkets and Asian food stores. To toast sesame seeds, stir seeds in a heavy-based frying pan over medium heat until lightly browned and fragrant.

do-ahead Recipe can be made, to the end of step 4, several hours ahead. Reheat in a single layer on large trays in a 180°C/350°F oven for 10 minutes before continuing at step 5.

ROASTED TOMATO
CHEESECAKES WITH OLIVES

PREP + COOK TIME 1 HOUR 10 MINUTES **MAKES** 8

4 MEDIUM VINE-RIPENED TOMATOES (600G), HALVED

1 TABLESPOON EXTRA VIRGIN OLIVE OIL

1½ CUPS (175G) LSA (SEE TIP)

30G (1 OUNCE) COLD BUTTER, CHOPPED

2 TEASPOONS WATER

1 TEASPOON FRESHLY GROUND BLACK PEPPER

250G (8 OUNCES) CREAM CHEESE, SOFTENED

2 EGGS

⅓ CUP (60G) SICILIAN GREEN OLIVES

60G (2 OUNCES) BABY SPINACH

1 Preheat oven to 180°C/350°F. Line a shallow-sided oven tray with baking paper. Place tomatoes, cut-side up, on tray; drizzle with oil, season. Roast tomatoes for 40 minutes. Pour any pan juices into a jug.

2 Meanwhile, grease eight 6cm (2½-inch) egg rings.

3 Pulse LSA, butter, water and pepper in a small food processor until ingredients come together. Divide mixture into eight portions; press firmly into rings. Refrigerate until required.

4 Beat cream cheese in a small bowl with an electric mixer for 2 minutes or until smooth. Beat in eggs, one at a time; season. Spoon cheese mixture into tins. Lightly press one tomato half on top of each cheesecake.

5 Bake cheesecakes for 20 minutes or until golden brown and slightly puffed.

6 Meanwhile, press olives with the side of a large knife blade; remove seeds. Chop olives finely. Add olives to reserved pan juices; season to taste.

7 Just before serving, spoon olive mixture over cheesecakes; serve warm with spinach leaves.

nutritional count per cheesecake 31g total fat (11g saturated fat); 1417kJ (339 cal); 3g carbohydrate; 11g protein; 6g fibre

tip LSA is a mixture of ground linseeds, sunflower seeds and almonds. It's available from some large supermarkets and health food stores.

serving suggestion Serve cheesecakes with rocket, a green leafy salad or steamed asparagus.

SWEET POTATO & PROSCIUTTO SPIRAL TART

PREP + COOK TIME 1 HOUR 30 MINUTES **SERVES** 4

30G (1 OUNCE) BUTTER

2 LARGE ONIONS (400G), SLICED

2 EGGS, SEPARATED

½ CUP (90G) CANNED CANNELLINI BEANS, RINSED

½ TEASPOON BAKING POWDER

½ CUP (60G) ALMOND MEAL

2 TABLESPOONS CURRANTS

⅓ CUP (55G) NATURAL ALMONDS, CHOPPED

⅓ CUP (10G) CHOPPED FRESH SAGE LEAVES, CHOPPED FINELY

800G (1½ POUNDS) ORANGE SWEET POTATOES, SLICED 2MM (⅛-INCH) THICK LENGTHWAYS

1 TABLESPOON EXTRA VIRGIN OLIVE OIL

200G (6½ OUNCES) SHAVED PROSCIUTTO

12 FRESH SAGE LEAVES, EXTRA

COOKING-OIL SPRAY

1 Preheat oven to 200°C/400°F. Grease a 20cm (8-inch) springform cake pan; line base and side with baking paper. Place on an oven tray.

2 Heat butter in a medium frying pan over medium heat; cook onion, stirring occasionally, for 15 minutes or until caramelised. Process caramelised onion, egg yolks, beans and baking powder until smooth. Season to taste. Transfer mixture to a large bowl. Whisk egg whites in a small bowl with an electric mixer until firm peaks form. Fold almond meal into onion mixture; gently fold in egg white in two batches. Spread onion mixture into cake pan; level surface.

3 Combine currants, chopped almonds and chopped sage in a small bowl.

4 Brush sweet potato slices with oil. Lay a slice of sweet potato on a clean work surface; top with a slice of prosciutto. Roll into a spiral and stand, spiral-side up, on onion base. Press lightly into base to secure roll. Repeat with remaining sweet potato and prosciutto. Sprinkle with currant mixture.

5 Bake tart, covered with foil, for 30 minutes. Remove foil. Bake tart for further 30 minutes or until top is crisp and sweet potato is tender. Spray extra sage leaves with oil; add to oven tray for the last 10 minutes of baking. Arrange leaves over tart before serving.

nutritional count per serving 41.1g total fat (10.2g saturated fat); 2814kJ (672 cal); 40.8g carbohydrate; 31g protein; 14g fibre
serving suggestion Serve tart with mixed salad leaves dressed with a simple vinaigrette. To make vinaigrette, add 1 teaspoon dijon mustard, 1 tablespoon lemon juice and ¼ cup olive oil to a screw-top jar. Season; shake well before serving.

CAPRESE PORTABELLO MUSHROOM PIZZAS

PREP + COOK TIME 40 MINUTES **SERVES** 4

12 FLAT MUSHROOMS (960G), TRIMMED

1 TABLESPOON EXTRA VIRGIN OLIVE OIL

500G (1 POUND) TOMATOES, SLICED THICKLY

3 BUFFALO MOZZARELLA (390G), DRAINED, SLICED

80G (2½ OUNCES) ROCKET (ARUGULA)

BASIL & MINT PESTO

⅔ CUP FIRMLY PACKED FRESH BASIL LEAVES

⅔ CUP FIRMLY PACKED FRESH MINT LEAVES

2 CLOVES GARLIC, PEELED, HALVED

2 TABLESPOONS GRATED PECORINO CHEESE

1 TABLESPOON PINE NUTS

⅓ CUP (80ML) EXTRA VIRGIN OLIVE OIL

1 Preheat oven to 190°C/375°F. Line an oven tray with baking paper. Place a wire rack on tray.

2 Place mushrooms on wire rack, stem-side up. Brush with oil; season. Bake for 15 minutes or until softened slightly.

3 Meanwhile, make basil and mint pesto.

4 Top mushrooms with tomato and mozzarella; bake for a further 5 minutes or until mozzarella softens lightly. Drizzle pizzas with pesto; serve with any remaining pesto.

basil & mint pesto Blend or process all ingredients until just combined. Season to taste.

nutritional count per serving 57g total fat (22g saturated fat); 2729kJ (652 cal); 4g carbohydrate; 26g protein; 7g fibre

tip Buffalo mozzarella is available from some large supermarkets and delis. You can use bocconcini instead.

do-ahead Pesto can be made a day ahead. Keep tightly covered with plastic wrap on the surface in the fridge.

JALAPEÑO & ROAST CAPSICUM BEEF POT PIES

PREP + COOK TIME 50 MINUTES **SERVES** 4

2 TABLESPOONS EXTRA VIRGIN OLIVE OIL

1 MEDIUM ONION (150G), CHOPPED FINELY

500G (1 POUND) MINCED (GROUND) BEEF

12 CLOVES GARLIC, CRUSHED

¼ CUP CHOPPED FRESH OREGANO LEAVES

¾ CUP (180G) CHOPPED DRAINED ROASTED RED CAPSICUMS (BELL PEPPERS)

½ CUP (60G) PICKLED JALAPEÑO, DRAINED, CHOPPED COARSELY

2 TABLESPOONS PLAIN (ALL-PURPOSE) FLOUR

1½ TABLESPOONS TOMATO PASTE

1½ TABLESPOONS WORCESTERSHIRE SAUCE

2 CUPS (500ML) BEEF STOCK

2 TEASPOONS CUMIN SEEDS

CREAM CHEESE PASTRY

60G (2 OUNCES) CREAM CHEESE, CHOPPED

1½ CUPS (150G) GRATED MOZZARELLA

1 CUP (120G) ALMOND MEAL

1 TEASPOON GARLIC POWDER

1 EGG

SMOKY HOT SAUCE

1 CUP (240G) ROASTED RED CAPSICUM (PEPPER) IN OIL, DRAINED

2 TEASPOONS TABASCO SAUCE

1 TEASPOON SMOKED PAPRIKA

1 Make cream cheese pastry.

2 Preheat oven to 200°C/400°F. Lightly grease four 1-cup (250ml) ovenproof dishes. Place dishes on an oven tray.

3 Heat the oil in a large saucepan over high heat. Cook the onion, beef, garlic and oregano for 10 minutes, stirring constantly, breaking up any lumps with a wooden spoon, until browned.

4 Add the capsicum, jalapeños and flour. Cook, stirring, for 1 minute. Add the tomato paste, worcestershire sauce and stock. Cook, stirring occasionally, for 5 minutes or until thickened. Season to taste. Spoon into dishes.

5 Roll cream cheese pastry between sheets of baking paper to 5mm (¼-inch) thick. Cut out four 11cm (4½-inch) rounds. Place rounds on top of pies; press edges with a fork. Sprinkle tops with cumin seeds. Bake for 15 minutes or until pastry is golden and crisp.

6 Meanwhile, make smoky hot sauce.

7 Serve pies with smoky hot sauce.

cream cheese pastry Place cream cheese and mozzarella in a microwave-safe bowl. Microwave on HIGH (100%) for 1 minute, stir; microwave for a further 1 minute or until melted. Stir in the almond meal, garlic powder and egg; season to taste. If the dough gets too stringy to work with, microwave for a further 30 seconds. Cover.

smoky hot sauce Process all ingredients until smooth; season to taste.

nutritional count per serving 59g total fat (17.4g saturated fat); 3367kJ (804 cal); 15.8g carbohydrate; 49.7g protein; 7g fibre

tips We tested the pastry in a 900-watt microwave oven. Ovens with higher wattage will take less time. If you don't like spicy food, use more capsicum and less jalapeños.

do-ahead You can make the beef filling a day ahead; spoon into dishes, cover and refrigerate.

BLACKBERRY, RICOTTA & ROCKET PIZZA

PREP + COOK TIME 55 MINUTES **SERVES** 4

2 CUPS (240G) ALMOND MEAL, TOASTED (SEE TIPS)

¼ TEASPOON BAKING POWDER

2 EGGS, BEATEN LIGHTLY

¼ CUP (60ML) EXTRA VIRGIN OLIVE OIL

1 CLOVE GARLIC, CRUSHED

1 TABLESPOON DRIED SPAGHETTI HERBS (SEE TIPS)

1 TABLESPOON EXTRA VIRGIN OLIVE OIL, EXTRA

1 LARGE ONION (200G), SLICED THINLY

1 CUP (240G) REDUCED-FAT RICOTTA (SEE TIPS)

120G (4 OUNCES) MOZZARELLA, CUT INTO 5MM (¼-INCH) SLICES

200G (6½ OUNCES) BLACKBERRIES (SEE TIPS)

60G (2 OUNCES) ROCKET (ARUGULA)

1 Preheat oven to 200°C/400°F. Line two 25cm (10-inch) round pizza trays with baking paper.

2 Combine almond meal and baking powder in a large bowl. Make a well in the centre; add egg, ¼ cup of the oil, garlic and herbs. Mix to form a soft, sticky dough.

3 Divide dough in half. Shape each half into a disc. Using damp hands, gently press out dough to fit trays. Drizzle with remaining oil; season. Bake in the hottest part of the oven for 15 minutes until lightly golden. Cool.

4 Meanwhile, heat the extra oil in a small non-stick frying pan over medium-high heat. Cook onion, stirring, for 2 minutes or until softened. Reduce heat to low; cook for 15 minutes, stirring occasionally, or until golden and caramelised.

5 Increase oven to 220°C/425°F. Spread pizza bases with ricotta and sprinkle with caramelised onion. Top with mozzarella; season.

6 Bake pizza for a further 10 minutes or until cheese is melted. Serve pizza immediately, topped with blackberries and rocket.

nutritional count per serving 65g total fat (11g saturated fat); 3154kJ (754 cal); 10g carbohydrate; 28g protein; 10g fibre

tips Toast almond meal in a 180°C/350°F oven for 8 minutes until lightly golden. Transfer immediately to a tray to cool. Spaghetti herbs are a mixture of dried basil, oregano, thyme, garlic, red pepper and parsley. You can substitute dried mixed herbs or Italian herbs. The consistency of ricotta varies between brands. If you find the ricotta is not soft enough to spread, whisk in a tablespoon of milk until smooth. If blackberries are out of season, use thawed frozen blackberries instead; drain well and pat dry on paper towel before using.

QUINOA CALZONES WITH RAINBOW SILVER BEET

PREP + COOK TIME 1 HOUR 20 MINUTES (+ REFRIGERATION & COOLING) **MAKES** 4

1½ CUPS (300G) WHITE QUINOA

2 TEASPOONS VEGETABLE STOCK POWDER

½ TEASPOON BAKING POWDER

3 EGGS

1 TABLESPOON EXTRA VIRGIN OLIVE OIL

20G (¾ OUNCE) UNSALTED BUTTER

1 SMALL ONION (80G), SLICED THINLY

2 CLOVES GARLIC, CRUSHED

1 BUNCH RAINBOW SILVER BEET (SWISS CHARD) (750G), CHOPPED COARSELY

½ CUP (125ML) POURING CREAM

¾ CUP (90G) GRATED SWISS CHEESE

1 TABLESPOON QUINOA FLAKES

1 Cook quinoa in a large saucepan of boiling salted water for 12 minutes or until tender; drain. Stand until cool enough to handle. Squeeze out excess water using hands. Process quinoa to a sticky paste. Add stock powder, baking powder, 2 eggs and the oil. Process using the pulse button until well combined. Turn dough out; knead lightly. Divide dough into four even portions. Roll each portion between sheets of baking paper until 20cm (8-inch) round and about 3mm (⅛-inch) thick. Slide dough, still in paper, onto a tray; refrigerate for 20 minutes or until firmer.

2 Meanwhile, preheat oven to 220°C/425°F. Line two large oven trays with baking paper.

3 Heat butter in a large frying pan until melted; cook onion and garlic, stirring, for 3 minutes or until softened. Add silver beet and cream; cook for 10 minutes or until wilted and almost dry. Cool. Squeeze out excess moisture. Transfer to a large bowl; season to taste. Stir in cheese.

4 Top each piece of dough with a quarter of the silver beet mixture. Fold rounds in half, pressing edges to enclose filling. Seal edges using a wet fork. Transfer calzones to trays. Lightly beat remaining egg; brush calzones with egg. Sprinkle with quinoa flakes.

5 Bake calzones for 30 minutes or until golden.

nutritional count per calzone 36g total fat (17g saturated fat); 2646kJ (632 cal); 48g carbohydrate; 26g protein; 9g fibre

do-ahead Calzones can be made 3 hours ahead, to the end of step 4. Keep covered in the fridge.

Big
SALADS

AVOCADO SALAD KALE WRAPS

PREP + COOK TIME 45 MINUTES (+ COOLING) **MAKES** 8

2 TABLESPOONS PEPITAS (PUMPKIN SEED KERNELS)

1 CUP (280G) GREEK-STYLE YOGHURT

3 TEASPOONS WASABI PASTE

16 BUTTER LETTUCE LEAVES

1 LEBANESE CUCUMBER (130G), PEELED INTO RIBBONS

½ CUP LOOSELY PACKED FRESH MINT LEAVES

70G (2½ OUNCES) SNOW PEA SHOOTS, TRIMMED

1 LARGE AVOCADO (320G), HALVED, SLICED

2 GREEN ONIONS (SCALLIONS), SLICED THINLY

KALE WRAPS

5 STEMS PURPLE KALE (200G), TRIMMED

2½ TABLESPOONS GREEK-STYLE YOGHURT

1½ TABLESPOONS LSA (SEE TIPS)

1 CUP (150G) CHICKPEA FLOUR (BESAN)

½ TEASPOON XANTHAN GUM

COOKING-OIL SPRAY

1 Make kale wraps.

2 Stir pepitas in a small dry frying pan over medium heat for 2 minutes.

3 Whisk yoghurt and wasabi in a small bowl until combined; season to taste.

4 Divide lettuce, cucumber, mint leaves, pea shoots, avocado and yoghurt mixture between wraps. Top with pepitas and green onion; roll up to enclose.

5 Serve immediately or wrap firmly in plastic wrap or foil to go.

kale wraps Pour boiling water over kale in a large heatproof bowl; stand for 1 minute, drain. Refresh in another bowl of iced water; drain. Place kale in a clean tea towel; squeeze out excess water. Process kale until finely chopped; return to large bowl. Add remaining ingredients, except oil spray; season. Mix with your hands to form a dough. Knead dough on a lightly floured surface until smooth. Divide dough into 8 portions; roll into balls. Cut two pieces of baking paper a little smaller than a large non-stick frying pan. Spray paper with cooking oil then roll out a ball between greased baking paper. Heat a large frying pan over a medium heat. As the wrap is very thin and fragile, peel one side of the paper away then place the wrap in the pan, paper-side up; cook for 30 seconds. Remove paper; turn wrap. Cook for a further 30 seconds. Repeat with remaining dough; cool. You will have 8 wraps in total.

nutritional count per wrap 13.2g total fat (3.3g saturated fat); 979kJ (234 cal); 16.3g carbohydrate; 9.7g protein; 5.5g fibre

tips LSA is a mixture of ground linseeds, sunflower seeds and almonds. It's available from some large supermarkets and health food stores. The wraps can be used in place of tortillas for burritos or soft tacos.

do-ahead These gluten-free kale wraps can be layered with baking paper and frozen in an airtight container or freezer bag for up to 2 months.

SAUCE VARIATIONS

Omit the wasabi in step 3 and instead combine the yoghurt with one of the following ingredients for different sauces:

beetroot 2 teaspoons finely grated beetroot.

spirulina 1 teaspoon spirulina.

turmeric 1 teaspoon ground turmeric.

INDIAN PANEER
& CHICKPEA SALAD

PREP + COOK TIME 25 MINUTES **SERVES** 4

250G (8 OUNCES) PANEER

1 TABLESPOON TANDOORI PASTE

200G (6½ OUNCES) SUGAR SNAP PEAS, TRIMMED

2 TABLESPOONS LEMON JUICE

2 TABLESPOONS EXTRA VIRGIN OLIVE OIL

400G (12½ OUNCES) CANNED CHICKPEAS (GARBANZO BEANS), DRAINED, RINSED

1 LARGE BEETROOT (BEETS) (200G), CUT INTO LONG THIN STRIPS (SEE TIPS)

2 MEDIUM CARROTS (240G), CUT INTO LONG THIN STRIPS (SEE TIPS)

1½ TABLESPOONS DRIED CURRANTS

⅓ CUP (50G) ROASTED UNSALTED CASHEWS

TURMERIC DRESSING

2 TABLESPOONS HULLED TAHINI

2 TABLESPOONS WARM WATER

1½ TABLESPOONS LEMON JUICE

1 TEASPOON HONEY

⅛ TEASPOON GROUND TURMERIC

1 Brush both sides of paneer with paste.

2 Place sugar snap peas in a large colander in the sink; pour boiling water over peas. Rinse under cold water; drain.

3 Combine juice and oil in a small jug; season.

4 Place chickpeas in a small bowl with half the juice mixture; mix well.

5 Make turmeric dressing.

6 Arrange sugar snap peas, beetroot, carrot, chickpeas and currants on a serving platter or bowls.

7 Cook paneer on a heated oiled grill plate (or grill or barbecue) over medium-high heat for 2 minutes each side or until lightly browned.

8 Add paneer to salad; top with cashews and remaining juice mixture. Serve with turmeric dressing.

turmeric dressing Combine ingredients in a small jug or bowl; season to taste. Adjust consistency of dressing with a little more warm water, if needed.

nutritional count per serving 35.1g total fat (9.8g saturated fat); 2439kJ (583 cal); 34.6g carbohydrate; 24g protein; 13.1g fibre

tips Use a julienne peeler to cut the beetroot and carrots into long thin strips. Julienne peelers are available from kitchenware stores and Asian food stores. When in season, add sliced fresh mango or grapes to the salad.

do-ahead Turmeric dressing can be made up to 3 days ahead. Store in a glass jar in the fridge.

GINGER BASIL CHICKEN WITH WATERMELON SALAD

PREP + COOK TIME 45 MINUTES (+ REFRIGERATION & STANDING) **SERVES** 4

¼ CUP (60ML) WHITE VINEGAR

½ CUP (125ML) EXTRA VIRGIN OLIVE OIL

1 CLOVE GARLIC, CRUSHED

1 TABLESPOON GRATED FRESH GINGER

½ CUP FIRMLY PACKED FRESH BASIL LEAVES, SHREDDED FINELY

4 X 250G (8-OUNCE) CHICKEN SUPREMES (SEE TIP)

600G (1¼ POUNDS) SEEDLESS WATERMELON, PEELED, CUT INTO LARGE WEDGES

4 BABY CUCUMBERS (120G), SLICED INTO RIBBONS

½ SMALL RED ONION (50G), SLICED THINLY

½ CUP (85G) DRY-ROASTED ALMONDS, CHOPPED

1 CUP LOOSELY PACKED FRESH MINT LEAVES

1 Process vinegar, oil, garlic, ginger and basil in a small food processor until smooth. Season to taste. Reserve half the basil mixture; cover, refrigerate.

2 Place chicken in a shallow non-reactive dish. Pour over the remaining basil mixture; cover, refrigerate for 1 hour.

3 Preheat oven to 200°C/400°F. Heat an ovenproof frying pan or flameproof baking dish over medium-high heat. Cook chicken, skin-side down, for 5 minutes or until skin is golden. Turn chicken; season. Transfer pan to the oven. Roast chicken for 12 minutes or until just cooked through. Transfer to a plate; cover loosely. Rest chicken for 10 minutes.

4 Arrange chicken on a platter with watermelon, cucumber, onion, almonds and mint. Drizzle with reserved basil mixture.

nutritional count per serving 77g total fat (16g saturated fat); 3765kJ (900 cal); 10g carbohydrate; 42g protein; 4g fibre

tip Chicken supremes are the boneless chicken breast fillets with skin attached and the first wing joint attached. You will need to order these from a butcher or poultry shop. You can use skinless chicken breast fillets instead, if you prefer.

do-ahead Recipe can be made 6 hours ahead, to the end of step 2.

CRISP FISH SALAD WITH BLOODY MARY DRESSING

PREP + COOK TIME 35 MINUTES **SERVES** 4

2 SMALL FENNEL BULBS (400G)

4 CELERY STALKS (600G), TRIMMED

600G (1¼ POUNDS) MIXED SMALL TOMATOES (TOMATO MEDLEY), SLICED THICKLY

2 TABLESPOONS EXTRA VIRGIN OLIVE OIL

4 X 150G (4½-OUNCE) WHITE FISH FILLETS, SKIN ON (SEE TIPS)

BLOODY MARY DRESSING

½ CUP (125ML) TOMATO JUICE

¼ CUP (60ML) EXTRA VIRGIN OLIVE OIL

2 TABLESPOONS FRESH LEMON JUICE

1 TABLESPOON HORSERADISH CREAM

½ TEASPOON CHILLI POWDER

½ TEASPOON CELERY SALT

½ TEASPOON WORCESTERSHIRE SAUCE

1 Reserve fennel fronds and the smaller celery leaves. Using a mandoline or V-slicer, thinly slice the fennel. Cut celery into long thin matchsticks. Combine fennel, celery and tomatoes on a large platter or on plates.

2 Make bloody mary dressing.

3 Heat oil in a large non-stick frying pan over high heat. Score fish skin; sprinkle with salt. Add fillets to pan, skin-side down, pressing down with a fish slice to prevent them from curling. Cook fillets for 5 minutes or until skin is crisp. Turn fillets; cook for a further 2 minutes or until just cooked through.

4 Serve fish with fennel salad, drizzled with bloody mary dressing. Top with reserved fennel fronds and celery leaves.

bloody mary dressing Whisk all ingredients in a small bowl until combined; season to taste. (Makes 1 cup)

nutritional count per serving 29g total fat (5g saturated fat); 1855kJ (443 cal); 9g carbohydrate; 33g protein; 5g fibre

tips We used snapper in this recipe, but any white fish fillet will be fine. Use the inner stalks of the celery for this recipe, if possible.

do ahead Bloody mary dressing can be made 3 days ahead.

GRILLED BABY OCTOPUS SALAD WITH QUINOA PANGRATTATO

PREP + COOK TIME 55 MINUTES (+ REFRIGERATION & COOLING) **SERVES** 4

1KG (2 POUNDS) BABY OCTOPUS, CLEANED

1 CUP (250ML) RED WINE VINEGAR

¼ CUP (60ML) EXTRA VIRGIN OLIVE OIL

4 CLOVES GARLIC, CRUSHED

3 TEASPOONS SMOKED PAPRIKA

4 MEDIUM ZUCCHINI (480G), CUT INTO 5MM (¼-INCH) SLICES LENGTHWAYS

400G (12½ OUNCES) GRAPE TOMATOES, HALVED

3 GREEN WITLOF (375G), LEAVES SEPARATED

QUINOA PANGRATTATO

½ CUP (100G) WHITE QUINOA

2 TEASPOONS EXTRA VIRGIN OLIVE OIL

1 FRESH LONG RED CHILLI, SEEDED, CHOPPED FINELY

2 TEASPOONS FINELY GRATED LEMON RIND

¼ CUP FINELY CHOPPED FRESH FLAT-LEAF PARSLEY

1 Rinse octopus well; drain. Pat dry with paper towel.

2 Combine vinegar, oil, garlic and paprika in a non-reactive bowl; season to taste. Add octopus; toss to combine. Cover; refrigerate for 1 hour.

3 Meanwhile, make quinoa pangrattato.

4 Preheat an oiled grill plate (or barbecue) over high heat. Cook the zucchini for 1 minute each side or until lightly browned. Drain the octopus over a bowl; reserve marinade. Cook octopus, turning once or twice, for 3 minutes or until just cooked through.

5 Pour reserved marinade into a small saucepan. Bring the marinade to the boil over a medium-high heat; simmer for 1 minute. Season to taste

6 Divide zucchini, tomatoes, witlof and octopus among plates. Drizzle with marinade and sprinkle with pangrattato.

quinoa pangrattato Rinse quinoa in a sieve; drain. Heat oil in a large heavy-based frying pan over medium low heat. Cook quinoa and chilli, stirring occasionally, for 25 minutes, or until golden and crisp. Transfer to a medium heatproof bowl; cool. Stir in rind and parsley; season to taste.

nutritional count per serving 23g total fat (4g saturated fat); 2064kJ (493 cal); 20g carbohydrate; 44g protein; 8g fibre

tip You can also use cuttlefish or small squid in the recipe.

do ahead Recipe can be made up to 3 hours ahead, to the end of step 3.

SALMON BLT WITH AMAZING GREEN SAUCE

PREP + COOK TIME 25 MINUTES **SERVES** 4

4 SKINLESS SALMON FILLETS (600G)

4 SLICES BACON (260G), RIND REMOVED

2 TEASPOONS EXTRA VIRGIN OLIVE OIL

400G (12½ OUNCES) MIXED SMALL TOMATOES (TOMATO MEDLEY), HALVED

2 BABY COS (ROMAINE) LETTUCE (360G), QUARTERED LENGTHWAYS

1 SMALL AVOCADO (200G), SLICED

AMAZING GREEN SAUCE

1 SMALL AVOCADO (200G), CHOPPED

½ CUP FIRMLY PACKED FRESH FLAT-LEAF PARSLEY LEAVES

¾ CUP FIRMLY PACKED FRESH CORIANDER (CILANTRO) LEAVES

¼ CUP (45G) PISTACHIOS

1 FRESH LONG GREEN CHILLI, CHOPPED

1 CLOVE GARLIC, CRUSHED

½ CUP (125ML) WATER

2 TABLESPOONS LIME JUICE

1 Make amazing green sauce.

2 Season salmon. Wrap each fillet with a bacon slice, secure with a toothpick. Heat oil in a large frying pan over medium heat. Cook salmon for 3 minutes each side or until browned and almost cooked through.

3 Place tomatoes, lettuce, avocado and salmon on a large platter. Serve with amazing green sauce.

amazing green sauce Blend or process all ingredients until smooth; season to taste. (Makes 2 cups)

nutritional count per serving 46g total fat (10g saturated fat); 2619kJ (626 cal); 6g carbohydrate; 45g protein; 6g fibre

do ahead The green sauce can be made up to a day ahead; keep tightly covered in the fridge.

HONEY-CHIPOTLE CHICKEN & AVOCADO BURRITO BOWL

PREP + COOK TIME 50 MINUTES **SERVES** 4

2 CHIPOTLE CHILLIES IN ADOBO SAUCE (35G), CHOPPED FINELY

1 CLOVE GARLIC, CRUSHED

1 TABLESPOON FINELY GRATED LEMON RIND

1 TABLESPOON HONEY

2 TABLESPOONS EXTRA VIRGIN OLIVE OIL

4 CHICKEN BREAST FILLETS (800G), HALVED LENGTHWAYS

½ CUP (100G) WHITE QUINOA

1 CUP (250ML) WATER

2 CORN COBS (500G), HUSKS AND SILKS REMOVED

250G (8 OUNCES) CHERRY TOMATOES, HALVED

4 GREEN ONIONS (SCALLIONS) (100G), SLICED

1 LARGE AVOCADO (320G), SLICED

1 CUP FIRMLY PACKED FRESH CORIANDER (CILANTRO) LEAVES

CHIPOTLE DRESSING

¼ CUP (60ML) FRESH LEMON JUICE

2 TABLESPOONS EXTRA VIRGIN OLIVE OIL

1½ TABLESPOONS RED WINE VINEGAR

1 SMALL CLOVE GARLIC, CRUSHED

1 Reserve 1 teaspoon of adobo sauce for the dressing. Combine chipotle chillies, garlic, rind, honey and oil in a large bowl. Add chicken; turn to coat in oil mixture.

2 Rinse quinoa in a sieve; drain. Place quinoa and the water in a small saucepan; bring to the boil. Reduce heat; cook, covered, over low heat for 15 minutes or until tender and liquid absorbed.

3 Meanwhile, make chipotle dressing.

4 Cook corn on a heated grill plate (or barbecue) over high heat for 12 minutes, turning occasionally, or until blackened and tender.

5 Reduce heat to low, cook chicken for about 3 minutes each side or until cooked through.

6 Combine quinoa, corn, tomatoes , green onion, avocado and coriander in a large bowl; drizzle with half the dressing. Divide salad among bowls, top with chicken; drizzle with remaining dressing. Serve with lime wedges, if you like.

chipotle dressing Combine all ingredients and reserved adobo sauce in a small bowl; season to taste.

nutritional count per serving 39g total fat (7g saturated fat); 2963kJ (708 cal); 32g carbohydrate; 53g protein; 10g fibre

tips You can use prawns instead of chicken; you will need about 1kg (2 pounds) whole prawns in shells or 500g (1 pound) peeled prawns.

do-ahead Recipe can be made up to 4 hours ahead, to the end of step 3.

MEDITERRANEAN BEEF & FARRO SALAD

PREP + COOK TIME 50 MINUTES **SERVES** 4

½ CUP (100G) FARRO (SEE TIPS)

1¼ CUPS (310ML) WATER

¼ CUP (60ML) RED WINE VINEGAR

2 CLOVES GARLIC, CRUSHED

¼ CUP LOOSELY PACKED FRESH MARJORAM LEAVES, CHOPPED COARSELY

¼ CUP (60ML) EXTRA VIRGIN OLIVE OIL

900G (1¾ POUNDS) RUMP STEAKS

280G (9 OUNCES) ARTICHOKE HEARTS IN OIL, DRAINED, QUARTERED

⅓ CUP (40G) SICILIAN GREEN OLIVES, PITTED, HALVED

250G (8 OUNCES) SMALL HEIRLOOM TOMATOES, SLICED

½ CUP (120G) ROASTED CAPSICUM (BELL PEPPER), TORN INTO THICK STRIPS

1 CUP (250G) CANNED CANNELLINI BEANS, RINSED

60G (2 OUNCES) BABY SPINACH LEAVES

ALMOND & CAPSICUM PESTO

½ CUP (120G) ROASTED CAPSICUM (BELL PEPPER)

½ CUP (80G) NATURAL ALMONDS, ROASTED

½ CUP (40G) GRATED PARMESAN

1 CLOVE GARLIC, CRUSHED

2 TABLESPOONS EXTRA VIRGIN OLIVE OIL

2 TEASPOONS RED WINE VINEGAR

1 Combine farro and the water in a small saucepan; bring to the boil. Reduce heat to low; cook, covered, for 45 minutes or until just tender. Drain.

2 Meanwhile, combine red wine vinegar, garlic, marjoram and 1½ tablespoons of the oil in a large bowl; season to taste. Add the steaks; turn to coat in marinade. Stand steaks at room temperature for 30 minutes before cooking.

3 Meanwhile, make almond and capsicum pesto.

4 Drain steak from marinade. Cook steak on a heated grill plate (or barbecue) over high heat for 2 minutes each side for medium, or until cooked to your liking (see tips). Remove from heat; rest, covered loosely, for 5 minutes.

5 Place farro and half the pesto in a large bowl with artichokes, olives, tomato, capsicum, beans, spinach and remaining oil; toss to combine, season. Divide among bowls. Thinly slice steak. Place steak on salad; top with remaining pesto.

almond & capsicum pesto Blend or process all ingredients until smooth; season to taste.

nutritional count per serving 57g total fat (10g saturated fat); 4071kJ (972 cal); 36.4g carbohydrate; 74.8g protein; 12.8g fibre

tips Farro is the whole spelt grain; it's available from health food stores. You can use barley, brown rice or green lentils instead. The cooking time of the rump steak will depend on the thickness and the temperature; try to let the steak stand at room temperature before cooking for more even results. This pesto is also great in tarts, on pizzas and with crostini.

do-ahead The steak can be marinated for up to 1 hour; avoid marinating for longer, as the vinegar will change the texture. If marinating for 1 hour, refrigerate the steak for the first 30 minutes and stand at room temperature for the next 30 minutes. Farro can be cooked and pesto made several hours ahead. Keep tightly covered in the fridge.

POACHED CHICKEN & WINTER GREEN SALAD

PREP + COOK TIME 45 MINUTES (+ STANDING) **SERVES** 4

1 BUNCH FRESH CORIANDER (CILANTRO) (130G)

1 MEDIUM LEMON (140G)

1 TABLESPOON FINELY CHOPPED FRESH LEMON GRASS

1 TEASPOON FINE SEA SALT

4 CHICKEN BREAST FILLETS (800G)

2 MEDIUM ZUCCHINI (240G), QUARTERED LENGTHWAYS

2 LEBANESE CUCUMBERS (260G), QUARTERED LENGTHWAYS

2 BUNCHES BROCCOLINI (350G), TRIMMED

455G (14½ OUNCES) FROZEN EDAMAME (SOYBEANS)

2 GREEN WITLOF, LEAVES SEPARATED

¾ CUP (120G) BLANCHED ALMONDS, ROASTED, CHOPPED COARSELY

GREEN CHILLI DRESSING

4 FRESH LONG GREEN CHILLIES, HALVED, SEEDED

1 TABLESPOON FINELY CHOPPED FRESH CORIANDER (CILANTRO) LEAVES

½ TEASPOON GROUND CUMIN

1 TEASPOON PURE MAPLE SYRUP

2 TABLESPOONS FRESH LIME JUICE

⅓ CUP (80ML) EXTRA VIRGIN OLIVE OIL

1 Wash coriander well; drain, pat dry. Remove leaves from coriander; reserve. Finely grate the rind from the lemon; squeeze the juice from the lemon. You will need ¼ cup (60ml) juice. Fill a large saucepan with water; add the coriander stems, juice, lemon grass and salt. Bring to the boil; add chicken. Return to the boil, cover with a lid; remove from heat. Stand for 20 minutes.

2 Meanwhile, cook zucchini, cucumber and broccolini on a heated oiled grill plate (or barbecue) until charred lightly.

3 Make green chilli dressing.

4 Cook edamame in a small saucepan of boiling water for 5 minutes. Drain; rinse under cold water. Remove beans from pods; transfer to a large bowl. Add lemon rind, charred vegetables, witlof and almonds; mix to combine.

5 Remove chicken from pan; shred or slice thinly. Add chicken to salad; spoon over chilli dressing. Top with reserved coriander sprigs to serve.

green chilli dressing Cook chilli on a heated oiled grill plate (or barbecue) until charred lightly. Chop chilli finely. Place chilli in a small bowl with the remaining ingredients; stir to combine. Season to taste.

nutritional count per serving 44.8g total fat (5.2g saturated fat); 3047kJ (728 cal); 13g carbohydrate; 61.2g protein; 9.4g fibre

tip You could swap any of the grilled greens in this recipe with asparagus, beans or asian greens.

do-ahead The dressing can be made 3 hours ahead.

QUINOA CRISP FATTOUSH WITH SEARED LAMB

PREP + COOK TIME 1 HOUR 10 MINUTES **SERVES** 4

⅓ CUP (80ML) OLIVE OIL

1 TEASPOON RAS EL HANOUT

400G (12½ OUNCES) LAMB BACKSTRAPS, TRIMMED

1 CUP FIRMLY PACKED FRESH FLAT-LEAF PARSLEY LEAVES

250G (8 OUNCES) CHERRY TOMATOES, HALVED

6 RED RADISHES (210G), SLICED THINLY

½ MEDIUM RED ONION (85G), SLICED THINLY

2 BABY COS (ROMAINE) LETTUCE (360G), LEAVES SEPARATED

½ CUP LOOSELY PACKED FRESH MINT LEAVES

½ CUP LOOSELY PACKED FRESH MARJORAM LEAVES

2 TABLESPOONS FRESH LEMON JUICE

1 CLOVE GARLIC, CRUSHED

QUINOA CRISP

⅓ CUP (65G) WHITE QUINOA

2 TABLESPOONS BLACK CHIA SEEDS

2 TABLESPOONS LINSEEDS (FLAXSEEDS)

1 TABLESPOON EXTRA VIRGIN OLIVE OIL

1 CUP (250ML) WATER

⅓ CUP (25G) FINELY GRATED PARMESAN

1 Make quinoa crisp.

2 Meanwhile, combine 1 tablespoon of the oil and ras el hanout in a medium bowl. Add the lamb; turn to coat. Stand at room temperature while preparing the salad.

3 Combine the parsley, tomato, radish, onion, lettuce and herbs in a large bowl. Whisk juice, remaining oil and garlic in a small bowl; season to taste.

4 Cook lamb on a heated grill plate (or barbecue) over a high heat for 3 minutes each side for medium, or until cooked as desired. Transfer lamb to a plate; season with sea salt. Rest lamb, covered loosely, for 5 minutes.

5 Arrange the salad on a platter; drizzle with dressing. Slice lamb thinly; add to salad with quinoa crisp.

quinoa crisp Preheat oven to 180°C/350°F. Line an oven tray with baking paper. Combine the quinoa, chia seeds, linseeds, oil and the water in a small saucepan. Stir over a medium heat for 3 minutes until the mixture begins to pull away from the side of the pan and has formed a thick consistency. Add the parmesan; stir for a further 2 minutes. Remove from heat; season. Spread mixture thinly over the tray. Cover with a second sheet of baking paper; roll out to a thickness of 5mm (¼-inch). Bake for 20 minutes, remove paper; bake for a further 20 minutes. Carefully turn the crisp over; bake for another 20 minutes or until golden brown and crisp. Cool. Break into pieces.

nutritional count per serving 47g total fat (8g saturated fat); 2556kJ (611 cal); 17g carbohydrate; 40g protein; 12g fibre

tip If you prefer to serve the salad without the quinoa crisp, add a second piece of lamb.

do-ahead The quinoa crisp can be made a day ahead; store in an airtight container.

PORK FILLET SALAD
WITH MISO MAPLE DRESSING

PREP + COOK TIME 30 MINUTES **SERVES** 4

1 TABLESPOON GRATED FRESH GINGER

2 TABLESPOONS OLIVE OIL

1 TABLESPOON MIRIN

800G (1½ POUNDS) PORK FILLETS

200G (6½ OUNCES) KALE, SLICED THINLY

1 TABLESPOON FRESH LEMON JUICE

500G (1 POUND) SHREDDED RED CABBAGE

1 LARGE FENNEL BULB (550G), SLICED THINLY

2 TABLESPOONS SESAME SEEDS, TOASTED

¼ CUP MICRO HERBS, SUCH AS RED-VEIN SORREL

MISO MAPLE DRESSING

1 TABLESPOON WHITE (SHIRO) MISO

1 TABLESPOON PURE MAPLE SYRUP

1 TABLESPOON FRESH LEMON JUICE

2 TABLESPOONS OLIVE OIL

1 Preheat oven to 200°C/400°F. Combine ginger, 1 tablespoon of the oil and mirin in a medium bowl. Add pork; turn to coat.

2 Heat a non-stick frying pan over a high heat; cook the pork for 3 minutes or until golden brown all over. Transfer to an oven tray; roast for 15 minutes or until just cooked through. Rest pork, covered loosely, for 5 minutes.

3 Meanwhile, place kale in a large bowl; add juice and remaining oil. Season well; massage oil mixture into kale to soften it. Add cabbage, fennel and seeds.

4 Make miso maple dressing.

5 Place salad on a large plate. Slice pork; add to salad. Drizzle with miso maple dressing; top with micro herbs.

miso maple dressing Whisk all ingredients in a small bowl until combined.

nutritional count per serving 26.7g total fat (4g saturated fat); 2128kJ (508 cal); 14.4g carbohydrate; 48g protein; 8g fibre

tips Use a mandoline or V-slicer to finely slice the fennel. You can use fresh coriander leaves instead of the micro herbs. This dressing would work beautifully on Asian-style salads served with grilled fish.

do-ahead Dressing can be made a day ahead; keep refrigerated.

FRIED GOAT'S CHEESE, ENDIVE & APPLE SALAD

PREP + COOK TIME 35 MINUTES (+ REFRIGERATION) **SERVES** 4

300G (9½ OUNCES) SOFT GOAT'S CHEESE

2 SHEETS FILLO PASTRY

20G (¾ OUNCE) BUTTER, MELTED

1 RADICCHIO (200G), LEAVES SEPARATED, TORN

2 GREEN WITLOF (250G), LEAVES SEPARATED

60G (2 OUNCES) BABY SPINACH LEAVES

½ BUNCH CURLY ENDIVE (150G), LEAVES SEPARATED

1 MEDIUM GREEN APPLE (150G), QUARTERED, CORED, CUT INTO WEDGES

1 MEDIUM RED APPLE (150G), QUARTERED, CORED, CUT INTO WEDGES

⅓ CUP (80ML) VEGETABLE OIL

¼ CUP (25G) WALNUTS, ROASTED (SEE TIPS), CHOPPED COARSELY

1 TABLESPOON CHOPPED FRESH CHIVES

HONEY WALNUT DRESSING

¼ CUP (60ML) EXTRA VIRGIN OLIVE OIL

¼ CUP (60ML) RED WINE VINEGAR

1 TABLESPOON HONEY

1 CLOVE GARLIC, CRUSHED

2 TABLESPOONS CHOPPED FRESH CHIVES

2 TABLESPOONS WALNUTS, ROASTED, CHOPPED FINELY

1 Use wet hands to press cheese together into a 13cm (5¼-inch) round. Place one sheet of fillo pastry on a clean work surface; brush lightly with some of the butter. Top with remaining pastry; brush with butter. Place cheese on shorter end of pastry; fold over twice to enclose cheese. Tuck pastry under; press lightly to seal. Cover; refrigerate for 20 minutes.

2 Meanwhile, make honey walnut dressing.

3 Combine radicchio, witlof, spinach, endive and apple in a large bowl.

4 Heat oil in a small frying pan over medium-high heat. Fry cheese parcel for 1 minute on each side. Drain cheese parcel on paper towel.

5 Toss honey walnut dressing through salad. Serve cheese parcel with salad topped with walnuts and chives.

honey walnut dressing Place ingredients in a screw-top jar; shake well. Season to taste.

nutritional count per serving 54g total fat (17g saturated fat); 2711kJ (648 cal); 18g carbohydrate; 21g protein; 6g fibre

tips You can use soft fetta instead of goat's cheese. Witlof and endive are slightly bitter leaves; you can use a mixture of lettuce, radicchio, rocket or watercress instead. To roast walnuts, spread nuts onto an oven tray. Roast in 180°C/350°F oven for 5 minutes, or until nuts are golden brown. Or, place nuts in heavy-based frying pan; stir constantly over medium heat until they are browned lightly and fragrant. Use a frying pan around 14cm (5½-inch) diameter to fry the cheese parcel.

do-ahead The dressing, without the chives and walnuts, can be made 3 days ahead; add the chives and walnuts just before serving. The recipe can be made 3 hours ahead, to the end of step 3; keep refrigerated.

SWEET POTATO BEEF NACHOS

PREP + COOK TIME 1 HOUR 10 MINUTES **SERVES** 4

1 LARGE ORANGE SWEET POTATO (500G)

2½ TABLESPOONS EXTRA VIRGIN OLIVE OIL

1 TEASPOON SMOKED PAPRIKA

3 SMALL RED ONIONS (300G), SLICED THINLY

2 CLOVES GARLIC, CRUSHED

500G (1 POUND) MINCED (GROUND) BEEF

1 TABLESPOON MEXICAN SPICE MIX

½ CUP (85G) CANNED BLACK BEANS, RINSED

400G (12½ OUNCES) CANNED DICED TOMATOES

125G (4 OUNCES) BABY HEIRLOOM TOMATOES, HALVED

2 TABLESPOONS FRESH LIME JUICE

1 LARGE AVOCADO (320G), MASHED COARSELY

100G (3 OUNCES) FIRM FETTA, CRUMBLED

½ CUP LOOSELY PACKED FRESH CORIANDER (CILANTRO) LEAVES

1 MEDIUM LIME (90G), CUT INTO WEDGES

1 Preheat oven to 200°C/400°F. Line two large oven trays with baking paper.

2 Using a mandoline or V-slicer, cut sweet potato into very thin rounds. Combine 1 tablespoon of the oil and the paprika in a large bowl; season. Add sweet potato to bowl; toss to coat. Spread sweet potato in a single layer over trays. Bake for 25 minutes, turning halfway through cooking, or until chips are crisp.

3 Meanwhile, heat 1 tablespoon of the remaining oil in a large frying pan over medium heat. Cook two of the onions and the garlic for 8 minutes, stirring occasionally, or until onion is soft. Increase heat to high; add beef, cook, stirring occasionally, for 8 minutes or until beef is browned. Add spice mix; cook, stirring, for 1 minute or until fragrant. Add beans and canned tomatoes; bring to the boil. Reduce heat to low; simmer for 15 minutes or until thickened slightly. Season to taste; cover to keep warm.

4 Combine tomatoes and remaining onion in a medium bowl. Stir in remaining oil and 1 tablespoon of the lime juice; season.

5 Combine avocado and remaining lime juice in a small bowl; season to taste.

6 Spread beef mixture over a medium platter. Top with tomato and avocado mixtures, fetta and remaining coriander; season. Serve with sweet potato chips and lime wedges.

nutritional count per serving 42.6g total fat (13.4g saturated fat); 2880kJ (688 cal); 31g carbohydrate; 40g protein; 12g fibre

tip You can use canned red kidney beans instead of black beans, if you like.

do-ahead Beef mixture can be made up to one day ahead; keep covered in the fridge.

BEETROOT, LENTIL & GOAT'S CHEESE SALAD

PREP + COOK TIME 1 HOUR 15 MINUTES **SERVES** 4

4 LARGE BEETROOT (BEETS) (800G), WITH LEAVES

½ CUP (100G) FRENCH-STYLE GREEN LENTILS (SEE TIPS), RINSED

1 LITRE (4 CUPS) VEGETABLE STOCK

¼ CUP (60ML) EXTRA VIRGIN OLIVE OIL

2 TABLESPOONS RED WINE VINEGAR

1½ TABLESPOONS HONEY

400G (12½ OUNCES) PURPLE KALE

1 MEDIUM RADICCHIO (200G), TORN COARSELY

125G (4 OUNCES) GOAT'S CURD

½ CUP (50G) WALNUT HALVES, ROASTED, CHOPPED COARSELY

1 CUP LOOSELY PACKED FRESH PURPLE BASIL LEAVES

1 Trim leaves from beetroot; wash, dry and reserve leaves. You will need 2 cups (120g). Scrub beetroot well, place in a medium saucepan; cover with cold salted water. Bring to the boil over medium heat; reduce heat to low. Simmer, covered, for 1 hour or until tender. Drain. When beetroot are cool enough to handle, peel; cut into eight wedges each.

2 Meanwhile, place lentils and stock in a medium saucepan. Bring to the boil; cover with a tight-fitting lid. Reduce heat to low; simmer for 25 minutes or until tender. Drain.

3 To make the dressing, place 2 tablespoons of the oil, vinegar and honey in a small screw-top jar; shake well. Season to taste.

4 Remove kale leaves from stems; discard stems. Tear leaves coarsely. Heat remaining oil in a large wok or non-stick frying pan over high heat. Stir-fry reserved beetroot leaves and kale for 1 minute or until slightly wilted and tender. Combine beetroot, lentils, kale mixture and radicchio in a large bowl.

5 Place beetroot salad on a platter; drizzle with dressing. Top with spoonfuls of goat's curd; sprinkle with walnuts and basil.

nutritional count per serving 32g total fat (8g saturated fat); 2243kJ (536 cal); 35g carbohydrate; 20g protein; 12g fibre

tips French-style green lentils are Australian-grown and related to the famous French lentils du puy. These green-blue, tiny lentils have a nutty, earthy flavour and a hardy nature that allows them to be rapidly cooked without disintegrating. You can use Persian fetta in place of goat's curd.

do-ahead Beetroot, lentils and dressing can be prepared a day ahead. Serve cold, or reheat beetroot and lentils before starting at step 4 for a warm salad.

KOREAN BEEF SALAD WITH KIMCHI CRUNCH SLAW

PREP + COOK TIME 25 MINUTES (+ REFRIGERATION & STANDING) **SERVES** 4

500G (1 POUND) THICK-CUT RUMP STEAK

2 TABLESPOONS EXTRA VIRGIN OLIVE OIL

2 TABLESPOONS GOCHUJANG (SEE TIPS)

¾ CUP (75G) KIMCHI (SEE TIPS), SHREDDED FINELY

2 CUPS (160G) SHREDDED RED CABBAGE

2 CUPS (340G) SHREDDED WOMBOK
(NAPA CABBAGE)

½ CUP (70G) ROASTED UNSALTED PEANUTS

1 TABLESPOON WHITE SESAME SEEDS, TOASTED

1 TABLESPOON BLACK SESAME SEEDS, TOASTED

½ CUP LOOSELY PACKED FRESH MINT LEAVES,
SHREDDED FINELY

1 MEDIUM LIME (90G), CUT INTO WEDGES

1 Combine steak, oil and gochujang in a shallow non-reactive dish. Cover; refrigerate for 2 hours or overnight.

2 Heat a large frying pan over high heat. Season steak well. Cook steak for 3 minutes each side for medium or until cooked to your liking. Transfer to a plate; rest, covered loosely, for 10 minutes.

3 Meanwhile, combine kimchi, cabbage, wombok, peanuts, seeds and mint in a large bowl.

4 Slice beef thinly against the grain; toss through salad with cooking juices. Season to taste.

5 Divide salad among four plates or bowls. Serve with lime wedges and extra kimchi, if you like.

nutritional count per serving 29.4g total fat (6.1g saturated fat); 1881kJ (449 cal); 10.6g carbohydrate; 33.2g protein; 5.2g fibre

tips Gochujang is a fermented Korean chilli paste that can be found in Asian supermarkets. Kimchi is a side dish of fermented vegetables, available from Asian supermarkets, some health food stores and delis.

pink grapefruit

turmeric dressing

green tahini

gorgonzola buttermilk

coriander lime

kalamata dressing

Dressings

These fresh and punchy dressings are perfect to elevate even the simplest of salads. But why stop there? Drizzle these dressing over a variety of proteins to add flavour to the most basic of dishes, taking your meat and three veg and adding an extra zing. The key is what the Italians call 'agrodolce', a balance of sweet and sour, and once you learn the ratio you like best, you can experiment with a range of different flavours.

PINK GRAPEFRUIT

prep time 15 minutes **makes** 1 cup

Segment 1 red grapefruit, by peeling rind thickly so no white pith remains. Cut between membranes, over a bowl to catch any juice, releasing segments. Reserve segments for salad. Squeeze 2 tablespoons juice from membrane into a small bowl. Add ¼ cup extra virgin olive oil, 1 finely chopped shallot, ½ cup pomegranate seeds and 1½ tablespoons red wine vinegar to bowl. Whisk to combine; season to taste.

goes well with seafood, pork and vegetables salads.

TURMERIC DRESSING

prep time 10 minutes **makes** ½ cup

Combine 2 tablespoons tahini, 2 tablespoons warm water, 1½ tablespoons lemon juice, 1 teaspoon honey and ⅛ teaspoon ground turmeric in a small jug or bowl; season. Adjust consistency of dressing with a little more warm water, if needed.

goes well with fish and vegetable salads.

GORGONZOLA BUTTERMILK

prep time 10 minutes **makes** 1 cup

Process 75g (2½ oz) mild gorgonzola and ½ cup buttermilk until smooth; season to taste. Stir in ⅓ cup toasted pine nuts and 2 tablespoons finely chopped fresh chives.

goes well with barbecued beef, pork, chicken or fish salads.

GREEN TAHINI

prep time 10 minutes **makes** ½ cup

Process ¼ cup tahini, ¼ cup fresh lemon juice, 2 tablespoons extra virgin olive oil, 2 tablespoons water, 1 small crushed clove garlic, 1 tablespoon fresh flat-leaf parsley leaves and 1 tablespoon basil leaves until smooth; season to taste.

goes well with fish, lamb and vegetable salads.

CORIANDER LIME

prep time 10 minutes **makes** ½ cup

Place 1 cup loosely packed fresh coriander (cilantro) leaves, 1 fresh coarsely chopped long green chilli, ¼ cup olive oil and 2 tablespoons lime juice in a blender or food processor; pulse until finely chopped. Season to taste.

goes well with kale, fish and char-grilled beef salads.

KALAMATA DRESSING

prep time 10 minutes **makes** ½ cup

Remove pits from ¼ cup kalamata olives. Finely chop olives and 1 small shallot. Combine with ¼ cup extra virgin olive oil, 2 tablespoons lemon juice and 1 teaspoon coarsely chopped fresh lemon thyme in a small bowl. Season to taste.

goes well with haloumi, seafood, lamb, beef and chicken salads.

LAMB & FREEKEH TABBOULEH WITH ZA'ATAR HALOUMI

PREP + COOK TIME 40 MINUTES **SERVES** 4

½ CUP (100G) CRACKED GREENWHEAT FREEKEH

3 CUPS (750ML) WATER

2 LEBANESE CUCUMBERS (260G), CHOPPED COARSELY

50G (1½ OUNCES) BABY KALE LEAVES

¼ CUP (40G) POMEGRANATE SEEDS

1½ CUPS LOOSELY PACKED FRESH FLAT-LEAF PARSLEY LEAVES, STEMS RESERVED

½ CUP LOOSELY PACKED FRESH DILL

400G (12½ OUNCES) LAMB LEG STEAKS

2 TABLESPOONS EXTRA VIRGIN OLIVE OIL

250G (8 OUNCES) HALOUMI, DRAINED

1 EGG, BEATEN LIGHTLY

¼ CUP (25G) ZA'ATAR

CUMIN DRESSING

⅓ CUP (80ML) EXTRA VIRGIN OLIVE OIL

¼ CUP (60ML) FRESH LEMON JUICE

1 TEASPOON GROUND CUMIN

½ CLOVE GARLIC, CRUSHED

1 Place freekeh in a small saucepan over high heat; cook for 1 minute, stirring, until lightly toasted. Add the water; bring to the boil. Simmer for 20 minutes or until just tender. Drain, rinse under cold water; drain well.

2 Meanwhile, make cumin dressing.

3 Combine freekeh, cucumber, kale and pomegranate in a large bowl. Finely chop 2 tablespoons of the parsley stems. Add to bowl with parsley leaves and dill leaves.

4 Season steaks. Heat half the oil in a large frying pan over high heat. Cook steaks for 3 minutes each side for medium, or until cooked to your liking. Transfer to a plate; rest, loosely covered, for 2 minutes.

5 Cut haloumi into 1cm (½-inch) thick slices. Cut slices in half diagonally. Pat haloumi slices dry with paper towel. Dip in egg; roll in za'atar to coat. Heat remaining oil in a large clean frying pan over high heat. Fry haloumi slices for 1 minute each side or until golden.

6 Toss salad with half of the dressing. Thinly slice lamb; place on top of salad with haloumi. Serve with remaining dressing.

cumin dressing Place ingredients in a small screw-top jar; shake well. Season to taste.

nutritional count per serving 51g total fat (14g saturated fat); 2988kJ (713 cal); 21g carbohydrate; 40g protein; 6g fibre

tips If you can't find cracked freekeh, use whole freekeh instead; it will require an extra 10 minutes cooking time to become tender. If you can't find za'atar, you can make your own: combine 2 tablespoons toasted sesame seeds, 1 tablespoon dried thyme, 2 teaspoons ground sumac and 2 teaspoons sea salt flakes.

do-ahead Freekeh and dressing can be prepared a day ahead; keep refrigerated.

CHAR-GRILLED BEEF, BROCCOLI & KALE SALAD

PREP + COOK TIME 40 MINUTES (+ STANDING) **SERVES** 4

600G (1¼ POUNDS) SKIRT STEAKS (SEE TIPS)

1KG (2 POUNDS) BROCCOLI, CUT INTO FLORETS, STEMS SLICED THINLY

2 TABLESPOONS EXTRA VIRGIN OLIVE OIL

¼ CUP (60ML) FRESH LEMON JUICE

¼ CUP (60ML) EXTRA VIRGIN OLIVE OIL, EXTRA

4 CLOVES GARLIC, CRUSHED

2 TEASPOONS GROUND SUMAC

2 TEASPOONS SMOKED PAPRIKA

2 TEASPOONS SEA SALT FLAKES

250G (8 OUNCES) KALE, STEMS REMOVED, LEAVES TORN

1½ CUPS LOOSELY PACKED FRESH FLAT-LEAF PARSLEY LEAVES

½ CUP (80G) SMOKED ALMONDS, CHOPPED COARSELY

1 MEDIUM LEMON (140G), CUT INTO WEDGES

1 Stand steak at room temperature for 15 minutes.

2 Meanwhile, place broccoli florets, stems, oil and half the juice in a large bowl; season. Toss to combine. Cook broccoli on a heated barbecue (or grill plate) over medium high heat for 4 minutes, turning occasionally, or until grill marks appear. Transfer to a large bowl.

3 Combine 1½ tablespoons of the extra oil with garlic, sumac and paprika in a small bowl. Pat steak dry with paper towel; rub with oil mixture. Sprinkle steak all over with the salt. Cook steak on heated barbecue (or grill plate) for 4 minutes each side for medium rare or until done to your liking. Transfer steak to a plate; rest, covered loosely, for 10 minutes. Slice steak thinly.

4 Meanwhile, to make dressing, place 3 teaspoons of the remaining extra oil and the remaining juice in a screw-top jar; shake well. Season to taste.

5 Heat the remaining extra oil in a large wok or frying pan over high heat. Cook kale, stirring, for 1 minute or until bright green and tender. Remove from heat.

6 Combine broccoli, steak, kale, parsley and dressing in a large bowl; season to taste. Arrange salad on a platter and sprinkle with almonds; serve with lemon wedges.

nutritional count per serving 51g total fat (10g saturated fat); 2873kJ (687 cal); 5g carbohydrate; 44g protein; 11g fibre

tips Skirt steak is a slightly chewy cut of beef, but has great flavour. The success in cooking this steak lies in allowing it to come to room temperature before cooking and resting well after cooking. Cook it to medium-rare, or medium at the most, and slice it thinly across the grain to serve. If you prefer a more tender cut, choose rump steak.

do-ahead Dressing can be made 2 days ahead; keep refrigerated.

ROAST SALMON WITH
SPICED CAULIFLOWER & SPINACH

PREP + COOK TIME 50 MINUTES **SERVES** 4

1.5KG (3 POUNDS) CAULIFLOWER, CUT INTO FLORETS

⅓ CUP (80ML) EXTRA VIRGIN OLIVE OIL

3 TEASPOONS GARAM MASALA

2 TEASPOONS GROUND TURMERIC

600G (1¼ POUNDS) SKINLESS, BONELESS SALMON FILLETS

180G (5½ OUNCES) BABY SPINACH LEAVES

200G (6½ OUNCES) BABY CUCUMBERS, SLICED THINLY LENGTHWAYS

½ CUP LOOSELY PACKED FRESH CORIANDER (CILANTRO) LEAVES

2 TABLESPOONS FRESH LEMON JUICE

½ CUP (140G) GREEK-STYLE YOGHURT

1 TABLESPOON WHITE SESAME SEEDS, TOASTED

2 TEASPOONS BLACK SESAME SEEDS

1 MEDIUM LEMON (140G), CUT INTO CHEEKS

1 Preheat oven to 200°C/400°F. Line two large oven trays with baking paper.

2 Toss cauliflower with half the oil, garam masala and turmeric in a large bowl; season. Divide cauliflower between trays. Roast for 20 minutes or until starting to brown.

3 Season salmon. Add salmon to trays with cauliflower. Roast for 5 minutes or until cauliflower is golden and salmon is almost cooked through. Transfer cauliflower to a large bowl; cool. Add spinach, cucumber and coriander to cauliflower in bowl. Break salmon into chunks.

4 To make dressing, place remaining oil and half the juice in a screw-top jar; shake well. Season to taste. Add dressing to salad; toss to combine.

5 Combine yoghurt and remaining juice in a small bowl; season to taste.

6 Divide salad and salmon among four plates, drizzle with yoghurt mixture; season to taste. Sprinkle with sesame seeds; serve with lemon cheeks.

nutritional count per serving 47g total fat (9g saturated fat); 2758kJ (659 cal); 12g carbohydrate; 42g protein; 11g fibre
tip Thinly slice cucumbers using a mandoline or V-slicer, or peel into ribbons with a vegetable peeler.
do-ahead The dressing and yoghurt mixture can be made a day ahead.

SMOKED RAINBOW TROUT SALAD

PREP + COOK TIME 25 MINUTES **SERVES** 4

2 FRESH LONG RED CHILLIES, SEEDED, CUT INTO LONG THIN STRIPS

1 CORN COB (250G), HUSKS AND SILKS REMOVED

600G (1¼ POUNDS) WHOLE HOT-SMOKED TROUT

3 CUPS (120G) FIRMLY PACKED TRIMMED WATERCRESS

½ CUP (100G) FROZEN SHELLED EDAMAME (SOYBEANS), THAWED (SEE TIPS)

6 RADISHES (200G), SLICED THINLY

WASABI DRESSING

½ CUP (150G) WHOLE-EGG MAYONNAISE

2 TABLESPOONS FRESH LEMON JUICE

½ CUP LOOSELY PACKED FRESH DILL

½ TEASPOON WASABI PASTE

1 Make wasabi dressing.

2 Place chilli in a bowl of iced water while preparing salad.

3 Cook corn on a heated grill pan (or barbecue) for 10 minutes or until charred all over and tender. Cool slightly; cut kernels from cob.

4 Meanwhile, remove skin and bones from trout; break flesh into chunks. Combine trout, corn, watercress, edamame and radish on a large platter.

5 Drizzle salad with wasabi dressing, top with drained chilli; season to taste. Serve with lemon wedges, if you like.

wasabi dressing Process all ingredients until smooth. Season to taste.

nutritional count per serving 36g total fat (5g saturated fat); 2126kJ (508 cal); 12g carbohydrate; 31g protein; 5g fibre

tips You will need about 200g (6½ ounces) of edamame in pods to get ½ cup (100g). For a shortcut, use a small drained can of corn kernels or frozen corn.

serving suggestion Serve salad with parsnip chips. Slice parsnips thinly on a mandoline or V-slicer. Drizzle with a little olive oil. Bake at 180°C/350°F for 30 minutes until golden and crisp.

SOUPS &
STEWS

LAMB & RED LENTIL CURRY

PREP + COOK TIME 2 HOURS 15 MINUTES **SERVES** 4

1 TABLESPOON COCONUT OIL

1 MEDIUM ONION (150G), SLICED THINLY

2 CLOVES GARLIC, CRUSHED

2CM (¾-INCH) PIECE FRESH GINGER (10G), CHOPPED FINELY

2 TEASPOONS GROUND CUMIN

2 TEASPOONS GROUND CORIANDER

1 TEASPOON GARAM MASALA

½ TEASPOON GROUND TURMERIC

1 CINNAMON STICK

700G (1½ POUNDS) DICED LAMB SHOULDER

1 TABLESPOON HONEY

400G (12½ OUNCES) CANNED DICED TOMATOES

1 LITRE (4 CUPS) BEEF STOCK

2 CUPS (500ML) WATER

2 SMALL ORANGE SWEET POTATO (500G), PEELED, CUT INTO 2CM (¾-INCH) PIECES

⅔ CUP (130G) RED LENTILS, RINSED

½ CUP (140G) GREEK-STYLE YOGHURT

⅓ CUP LOOSELY PACKED FRESH CORIANDER (CILANTRO) LEAVES

1 MEDIUM CARROT (120G), CUT INTO MATCHSTICKS

1 Heat coconut oil in a large saucepan over medium heat; cook onion, garlic, ginger and spices, stirring, for 2 minutes or until onion softens.

2 Add lamb; cook, stirring, for 3 minutes or until browned lightly. Stir in honey, tomatoes, stock and the water; bring to the boil. Reduce heat to low; simmer, covered, for 1½ hours or until lamb is just tender.

3 Stir in sweet potato and lentils; simmer, covered, for a further 15 minutes. Uncover; simmer for 5 minutes or until lamb, sweet potato and lentils are tender and sauce is thickened slightly. Season to taste.

4 Place yoghurt in a small bowl. Chop 1 tablespoon of the coriander finely; stir into yoghurt.

5 Serve curry topped with carrot, yoghurt mixture and remaining coriander.

nutritional count per serving 20.2g total fat (10.3g saturated fat); 2215kJ (529 cal); 45.3g carbohydrate; 36.3g protein; 9.8g fibre

do-ahead Curry can be made a day ahead. Thin with a little extra stock or water on reheating if the curry thickens. Curry can be frozen for up to 3 months, at the end of step 3.

serving suggestion Serve with cauliflower or broccoli rice, see page 179.

TORTILLA SOUP
WITH JICAMA CHIPS

PREP + COOK TIME 1 HOUR 30 MINUTES **SERVES** 4 (MAKES 10 CUPS)

1 TABLESPOON OLIVE OIL

1 MEDIUM ONION (150G), CHOPPED FINELY

2 CLOVES GARLIC, CRUSHED

1 JALAPEÑO CHILLI, SEEDED, CHOPPED FINELY

1 TEASPOON MEXICAN CHILLI POWDER

1 TEASPOON GROUND CUMIN

1 TEASPOON DRIED OREGANO

½ TEASPOON SMOKED PAPRIKA

800G (1½ POUNDS) CANNED DICED TOMATOES

1.5 LITRES (6 CUPS) VEGETABLE STOCK

400G (12½ OUNCES) CANNED BLACK BEANS, DRAINED, RINSED

1 LARGE AVOCADO (320G), DICED

¼ CUP COARSELY CHOPPED FRESH CORIANDER (CILANTRO) LEAVES

⅓ CUP (95G) GREEK-STYLE YOGHURT

1 MEDIUM LIME (90G), CUT INTO WEDGES

JICAMA CHIPS

500G (1 POUND) JICAMA (YAM BEAN)

½ TEASPOON GROUND TURMERIC

½ TEASPOON GROUND CUMIN

1 TEASPOON SEA SALT FLAKES

1 Make jicama chips.

2 Meanwhile, heat oil in a large heavy-based saucepan over medium heat. Cook onion, stirring occasionally, for 3 minutes or until softened. Add garlic and jalapeño; cook, stirring, for 2 minutes.

3 Add chilli powder, cumin, oregano and paprika; cook, stirring, for 1 minute or until fragrant. Stir in tomatoes and stock; bring to the boil. Reduce heat to low; simmer for 10 minutes. Add beans; simmer for a further 5 minutes. Season to taste.

4 Top soup with avocado, coriander, yoghurt and jicama chips; season to taste. Serve with lime wedges.

jicama chips Preheat the oven to 120°C/250°F. Line two oven trays with baking paper. Peel jicama. Using a mandoline or V-slicer, cut jicama into 3mm (⅛-inch) thin rounds. Pat dry well with paper towel. Place rounds in a single layer on oven trays; sprinkle with combined spices and salt. Roast in the oven for 1¼ hours or until crisp, swapping trays between shelves halfway through cooking time.

nutritional count per serving 20.5g total fat (4.7g saturated fat); 1818kJ (434 cal); 44.4g carbohydrate; 15g protein; 18.2g fibre

do-ahead Jicama chips can be made a day ahead; store in an airtight container. Soup can be made a day ahead, to the end of step 3.

GOAN FISH CURRY

PREP + COOK TIME 50 MINUTES **SERVES** 2

2 TEASPOONS GROUND CORIANDER

1 TEASPOON CUMIN SEEDS

2 DRIED CHILLIES

2 TABLESPOONS FINELY GRATED FRESH GINGER

4 CLOVES GARLIC, CRUSHED

1 TEASPOON GROUND TURMERIC

2 TABLESPOONS VEGETABLE OIL

1 LARGE ONION (200G), SLICED THINLY

4 MEDIUM ROMA (PLUM) TOMATOES (240G), CHOPPED FINELY

400ML (12½ OUNCES) CANNED COCONUT MILK

1 TABLESPOON FINELY GRATED PALM SUGAR

2 TEASPOONS TAMARIND PUREE

1 FRESH LONG GREEN CHILLI, SEEDED, CHOPPED FINELY

500G (1 POUND) FIRM WHITE FISH FILLETS, CUT INTO 4CM (1½-INCH) PIECES

100G (3 OUNCES) GREEN BEANS, CUT INTO 4CM (1½-INCH) LENGTHS

⅓ CUP LOOSELY PACKED FRESH CORIANDER (CILANTRO) LEAVES

1 Heat a large deep frying pan over medium heat. Cook ground coriander, cumin and dried chilli, stirring, for 1 minute or until fragrant. Using a spice grinder or a mortar and pestle, grind mixture until almost completely ground. Combine spice mixture with ginger, garlic and turmeric in a small bowl.

2 Heat oil in the same pan over medium heat. Cook onion, stirring occasionally, for 5 minutes or until starting to turn golden. Add spice mix; cook, stirring, for 2 minutes. Stir in tomato; cook, stirring, for 5 minutes or until most of the moisture is evaporated.

3 Stir in coconut milk, sugar, tamarind and fresh chilli; bring to the boil. Reduce heat to low; simmer for 5 minutes or until sauce is thickened slightly.

4 Add fish and beans to pan; simmer for 4 minutes or until just cooked through. Season to taste.

5 Serve curry topped with coriander leaves.

nutritional count per serving 39.7g total fat (16.3g saturated fat); 2964kJ (708 cal); 28.9g carbohydrate; 56g protein; 10.2g fibre

serving suggestion Serve with cauliflower rice, see page 179.

ZUCCHINI & PARMESAN SOUP WITH PARMESAN CRISPS

PREP + COOK TIME 45 MINUTES (+ STANDING)   **SERVES** 4 (MAKES 8 CUPS)

¼ CUP (60ML) OLIVE OIL

1KG (2 POUNDS) ZUCCHINI, QUARTERED LENGTHWAYS, CHOPPED COARSELY

2 CLOVES GARLIC, CRUSHED

⅓ CUP FIRMLY PACKED FRESH BASIL LEAVES, CHOPPED COARSELY

3 CUPS (750ML) VEGETABLE STOCK

¼ CUP (60ML) POURING CREAM

⅔ CUP (55G) GRATED PARMESAN

¼ CUP FRESH FLAT-LEAF PARSLEY LEAVES

PARMESAN CRISPS

1 CUP (80G) FINELY GRATED PARMESAN (SEE TIP)

2 TEASPOONS WHOLEMEAL PLAIN (ALL-PURPOSE) FLOUR

¼ TEASPOON FRESHLY GROUND BLACK PEPPER

1 TEASPOON FINELY CHOPPED FRESH ROSEMARY LEAVES

1 Heat the oil in a large heavy-based saucepan over low-medium heat. Cook zucchini and garlic, stirring occasionally, for 10 minutes or until zucchini is browned and very soft.

2 Meanwhile, make parmesan crisps.

3 Add basil and stock to pan; bring to the boil. Reduce heat to low; simmer for 8 minutes. Remove from heat; stand 5 minutes.

4 Blend or process three-quarters of the soup until smooth. Return soup to pan with cream and parmesan; stir over low heat until hot.

5 Sprinkle soup with parsley; season to taste. Serve with parmesan crisps.

parmesan crisps Preheat oven to 180°C/350°F. Line two oven trays with baking paper. Combine all ingredients in a medium bowl. Place 12 level tablespoons of mixture onto trays, flatten mounds to about 8cm (3¼ inches) across, leaving 5cm (2 inches) between rounds. Bake rounds for 6 minutes or until starting to turn golden. Lift one round at a time using a palette knife or metal spatula; drape over a rolling pin to cool.

nutritional count per serving 33g total fat (13g saturated fat); 1625kJ (388 cal); 6g carbohydrate; 16g protein; 3g fibre

tip When making the parmesan crisps, for best results use the fine side of a box grater rather than a Microplane-style grater when grating the parmesan.

do-ahead Soup can be made 6 hours ahead; keep refrigerated. Parmesan crisps can be made 2 days ahead; store in an airtight container.

SMOKY CAULIFLOWER & CORN CHOWDER

PREP + COOK TIME 35 MINUTES (+ STANDING) **SERVES** 4

1 CORN COB (250G), HUSK AND SILK REMOVED

¼ CUP (60ML) OLIVE OIL

1 MEDIUM ONION (150G), SLICED THINLY

2 CLOVES GARLIC, SLICED THINLY

1KG (2 POUNDS) CAULIFLOWER, CHOPPED

2 TEASPOONS SMOKED PAPRIKA

½ TEASPOON CAYENNE PEPPER

2 TABLESPOONS PLAIN (ALL-PURPOSE) FLOUR

1 LITRE (4 CUPS) CHICKEN STOCK

½ CUP (125ML) MILK

4 SLICES STREAKY BACON (120G), RIND REMOVED

½ CUP (60G) GRATED SMOKED CHEDDAR

⅓ CUP LOOSELY PACKED FRESH FLAT-LEAF PARSLEY LEAVES

1 Cut kernels from corn cob. Heat oil in a large saucepan over medium heat. Cook onion, garlic, cauliflower, corn, paprika and cayenne, stirring occasionally, for 10 minutes or until onion is softened. Add flour; cook, stirring, for 1 minute. Gradually stir in stock and milk; bring to the boil. Reduce heat to low; simmer for 10 minutes or until cauliflower is tender. Stand 10 minutes.

2 Blend soup in a food processor in batches using pulse button or use a hand-held stick blender until coarsely blended; season to taste. Return soup to pan; stir over medium heat until hot.

3 Meanwhile, cook bacon in a medium frying pan over high heat for 2 minutes each side or until browned and crisp. Drain on paper towel.

4 Divide soup among bowls. Top evenly with bacon, cheddar and parsley.

nutritional count per serving 29g total fat (9g saturated fat); 1712kJ (409 cal); 17g carbohydrate; 16g protein; 8g fibre

tip For a vegetarian version of this soup, omit the bacon and use vegetable stock.

do-ahead Recipe can be made up to 2 days ahead, to the end of step 2; keep refrigerated. Soup, without toppings, can be frozen for up to 2 months.

PICK-YOUR-PROTEIN CURRY

PREP + COOK TIME 30 MINUTES **SERVES** 4

2 TABLESPOONS VEGETABLE OIL

2 CLOVES GARLIC, CHOPPED

1 TABLESPOON GRATED FRESH GINGER

¼ CUP (75G) THAI RED CURRY PASTE

1 MEDIUM ORANGE SWEET POTATO (400G),
PEELED, GRATED COARSELY

1 CUP (250ML) CANNED COCONUT MILK

2 CUPS (500ML) STOCK OF CHOICE (SEE TIPS)

600G (1¼ POUNDS) PROTEIN OF CHOICE,
CUT INTO PIECES (SEE PICK-YOUR-PROTEIN)

100G (3 OUNCES) BROCCOLI, CUT INTO FLORETS

1 MEDIUM RED CAPSICUM (BELL PEPPER) (200G),
CHOPPED COARSELY

120G (4 OUNCES) GREEN BEANS, HALVED ON
THE DIAGONAL

½ CUP LOOSELY PACKED FRESH CORIANDER
(CILANTRO) LEAVES

1 MEDIUM LIME (90G), CUT INTO WEDGES

1 Heat oil in a large saucepan over low heat. Cook garlic, ginger, curry paste and sweet potato, stirring, for 5 minutes or until sweet potato is tender. Stir in coconut milk and stock. Blend or process in batches until smooth.
2 Return curry to pan; bring to a simmer. Add protein and vegetables; simmer for 5 minutes or until protein is cooked through and vegetables are just tender. Season to taste.
3 Sprinkle curry with coriander; serve with lime wedges.

pick-your-protein Here we used 600g (1¼ pounds) rump steak cut into thick slices. You could use the same weight of chopped skinless firm white fish fillets, sliced chicken breast fillets, sliced lamb backstrap (eye of loin), sliced pork scotch fillet or chopped tofu in this recipe. Simmer until the protein of choice is just cooked through.

nutritional count per serving
beef 20g total fat (7g saturated fat); 1879kJ (449 cal); 21g carbohydrate; 43g protein; 7g fibre
fish 19g total fat (6g saturated fat); 1718kJ (411 cal); 21g carbohydrate; 35g protein; 7g fibre
chicken 19g total fat (6g saturated fat); 1774kJ (424 cal); 21g carbohydrate; 31g protein; 7g fibre
lamb 24g total fat (8g saturated fat); 2123kJ (508 cal); 21g carbohydrate; 48g protein; 7g fibre
pork 18g total fat (6g saturated fat); 1702kJ (407 cal); 21g carbohydrate; 36g protein; 7g fibre
tofu 28g total fat (7g saturated fat); 1870kJ (447 cal); 21g carbohydrate; 23g protein; 12g fibre

tips You can use fish, chicken, beef or vegetable stock in this recipe, to suit the protein. You can add your favourite vegetables.
serving suggestion Serve with cauliflower or broccoli rice, see page 179.

BEAN, SILVER BEET & TOMATO STEW WITH ALMOND CRUMBLE

PREP + COOK TIME 1 HOUR 5 MINUTES **SERVES** 4

6 MEDIUM ROMA (PLUM) TOMATOES (360G), HALVED LENGTHWAYS

½ CUP (80G) NATURAL ALMONDS

2 TABLESPOONS OLIVE OIL

2 MEDIUM ONIONS (300G), CHOPPED FINELY

2 CLOVES GARLIC, CHOPPED FINELY

1 PINCH SAFFRON THREADS

½ TEASPOON CAYENNE PEPPER

2 SLICES BACON (130G), TRIMMED, CHOPPED FINELY

400G (12½ OUNCES) CANNED DICED TOMATOES

½ CUP (100G) FRENCH-STYLE GREEN LENTILS

2 CUPS (500ML) WATER

750G (1½ POUNDS) SILVER BEET (SWISS CHARD), TRIMMED, LEAVES CHOPPED

150G (4½ OUNCES) GREEN BEANS, TRIMMED, SLICED LENGTHWAYS

1 TABLESPOON FINELY GRATED LEMON RIND

½ CUP CHOPPED FRESH CURLY PARSLEY

30G (1 OUNCE) BUTTER

1 Preheat oven to 180°C/350°F. Line an oven tray with baking paper.

2 Place tomato halves, cut-side up, on lined tray; season generously with sea salt flakes and freshly ground black pepper. Roast for 30 minutes or until softened.

3 Meanwhile, spread almonds on a second oven tray; roast on a separate shelf with tomatoes for 10 minutes or until lightly browned and fragrant. Process almonds until coarsely chopped.

4 Heat oil in a large heavy-based saucepan. Add onion, garlic, saffron, cayenne pepper and bacon; cook, stirring, over medium heat for 5 minutes or until onion is softened and bacon is browned lightly. Add canned tomatoes, lentils and the water; simmer, covered, for 20 minutes.

5 Add silver beet in two batches; cook, covered, until first batch is wilted before adding the second batch. Stir well. Add beans and roasted tomatoes; simmer, covered, for a further 5 minutes or until beans are tender. Season to taste.

6 Place almonds, rind and parsely in a small heatproof bowl. Heat butter in a small saucepan over medium heat; cook, stirring, until it begins to brown. Pour over almond mixture; stir to combine.

7 Serve stew sprinkled with almond crumble.

nutritional count per serving 32g total fat (8g saturated fat); 2063kJ (493 cal); 24g carbohydrate; 20g protein; 14g fibre

tip For a vegetarian version, leave out the bacon.

serving suggestion Serve with four 40g slices sourdough bread for 41.9g carbohydrate per serve, or with 1½ cups cooked brown rice total for 45.4g carbohydrate per serve.

KALE & COCONUT SOUP
WITH COCONUT CRACKERS

PREP + COOK TIME 1 HOUR 45 MINUTES **SERVES** 4 (MAKES 8 CUPS)

2 TEASPOONS COCONUT OIL

1 MEDIUM LEEK (350G), TRIMMED, WHITE PART ONLY, CHOPPED COARSELY

2 CLOVES GARLIC, CHOPPED FINELY

½ TEASPOON GROUND CUMIN

¼ TEASPOON GROUND WHITE PEPPER

250G (8 OUNCES) KALE, TRIMMED, LEAVES CHOPPED, DISCARD STALKS

250G (8 OUNCES) ENGLISH SPINACH, TRIMMED, LEAVES CHOPPED

1 LITRE (4 CUPS) VEGETABLE STOCK

1 CUP (250ML) CANNED COCONUT MILK

⅓ CUP (80ML) CANNED COCONUT CREAM

COCONUT CRACKERS

1 EGG WHITE

¼ CUP (60ML) WATER

⅓ CUP (40G) ALMOND MEAL

⅓ CUP (50G) WHITE SESAME SEEDS

⅓ CUP (55G) LINSEEDS (FLAXSEEDS)

1¼ CUPS (100G) DESICCATED COCONUT

½ TEASPOON SEA SALT FLAKES

2 TABLESPOONS COCONUT OIL, MELTED

1 Make coconut crackers.

2 Meanwhile, heat the coconut oil in a large saucepan over medium-high heat. Cook leek, garlic, cumin and pepper for 5 minutes or until leek is soft but not coloured. Add kale and spinach; cook, covered, stirring occasionally, for 3 minutes or until wilted. Remove from heat.

3 Transfer kale mixture to a blender. Add 1½ cups of the stock; blend until smooth. Return kale mixture to same pan; stir in remaining stock and coconut milk. Season to taste; stir over medium heat until warmed through.

4 Ladle soup into warm bowls; top with a swirl of coconut cream. Season to taste; serve with coconut crackers.

coconut crackers Preheat oven to 160°C/325°F. Whisk egg white with the water in a medium bowl until soft peaks form. Stir in remaining ingredients until well combined, you may need to use your hands to bring mixture together. Divide mixture in half. Press one half between sheets of baking paper into a 20cm x 25cm (8-inch x 10-inch) rectangle. Repeat with remaining mixture. Transfer dough in paper onto oven trays; remove top layer of paper. Bake for 25 minutes. Swap trays in oven; bake for a further 25 minutes or until golden and firm. Cool on a wire rack. Break into large pieces.

nutritional count per serving 57g total fat (34g saturated fat); 2633kJ (629 cal); 10g carbohydrate; 15g protein; 16g fibre

tip If opening a small can of coconut cream to garnish, reserve the remainder, then add to a smoothie or curry, or drizzle over fruit salad.

do-ahead Coconut crackers can be made up to 1 week ahead; store in an airtight container. Soup can be made 6 hours ahead; keep refrigerated.

CHUNKY KALE & MEATBALL MINESTRONE

PREP + COOK TIME 1 HOUR 5 MINUTES (+ REFRIGERATION) **SERVES** 4

¼ CUP (60ML) EXTRA VIRGIN OLIVE OIL

1 MEDIUM ONION (150G), CHOPPED FINELY

1 MEDIUM CARROT (120G), CHOPPED FINELY

2 TRIMMED STALKS CELERY (200G), CHOPPED

2 X 400G (12½-OUNCE) CANS DICED TOMATOES

1 LITRE (4 CUPS) CHICKEN STOCK

400G (12½ OUNCES) CANNED CANNELLINI BEANS, DRAINED, RINSED

2 MEDIUM ZUCCHINI (240G), CHOPPED COARSELY

120G (4 OUNCES) KALE, TRIMMED, CHOPPED

1 MEDIUM LEMON (140G)

1 CLOVE GARLIC, CHOPPED FINELY

1 SMALL FENNEL BULB (200G), SLICED THINLY (SEE TIP)

HERBED MEATBALLS

⅓ CUP FRESH FLAT-LEAF PARSLEY LEAVES

2 TABLESPOONS FRESH BASIL LEAVES, SLICED THINLY

2 TABLESPOONS FRESH OREGANO LEAVES, CHOPPED FINELY

1 TABLESPOON FRESH ROSEMARY LEAVES, CHOPPED FINELY

500G (1 POUND) PORK AND VEAL MINCE

1 MEDIUM CARROT (120G), GRATED FINELY

¼ CUP (30G) ALMOND MEAL

2 TABLESPOONS TOMATO PASTE

1 EGG, BEATEN LIGHTLY

1 Make herbed meatballs.

2 Heat 1½ tablespoons of the oil in a large saucepan over a medium heat. Add onion; cook, stirring, for 5 minutes or until starting to soften. Add carrot and celery; cook, stirring, for 5 minutes or until softened. Add tomato, stock and beans; bring to the boil. Reduce heat to medium; cook, covered, for 20 minutes. Add zucchini and kale; cook for a further 5 minutes or until tender. Season to taste.

3 Meanwhile, heat remaining oil in a large frying pan over medium-high heat. Cook meatballs, in batches, until browned all over.

4 Add meatballs to the soup; simmer for a further 5 minutes or until meatballs are cooked through. Season to taste.

5 Grate rind from lemon and combine in the bowl with reserved parsley; add garlic and fennel. Serve soup topped with fennel mixture.

herbed meatballs Set 2 tablespoons flat-leaf parsley aside in a small bowl. Chop remaining parsley finely; combine with remaining ingredients in a medium bowl; season well. Roll mixture into 1 tablespoon balls; place on a tray. Refrigerate for 30 minutes.

nutritional count per serving 31.5g total fat (6.7g saturated fat); 2528kJ (604 cal); 29.1g carbohydrate; 40.5g protein; 16.7g fibre
tip Use a mandoline or V-slicer to thinly slice the fennel.
do-ahead Meatballs can be made a day ahead; keep covered in the fridge, or freeze for up to 3 months.
serving suggestion You can also serve the soup with four 50g slices wholemeal sourdough bread for 33.6g carbohydrate per serve.

ONION SOUP WITH CHEESY SWEET POTATO TOASTS

PREP + COOK TIME 1 HOUR 30 MINUTES **SERVES** 4

2 TABLESPOONS OLIVE OIL

1 LARGE LEEK (500G), SLICED THINLY

2 LARGE RED ONIONS (600G), SLICED THINLY

2 LARGE ONIONS (400G), SLICED THINLY

3 CLOVES GARLIC, CRUSHED

1 TABLESPOON FRESH THYME LEAVES

1.5 LITRES (6 CUPS) BEEF STOCK

1 TABLESPOON RED WINE VINEGAR

CHEESY SWEET POTATO TOASTS

2 SMALL ORANGE SWEET POTATOES (500G), CUT INTO 1CM (½-INCH) THICK SLICES ON THE DIAGONAL

1 TABLESPOON OLIVE OIL

2 TABLESPOONS PESTO

⅓ CUP (40G) COARSELY GRATED GRUYÈRE CHEESE

1 Heat oil in a large saucepan over high heat. Add leek and onions; reduce heat to low. Cook, covered, stirring occasionally, for 45 minutes or until onion is caramelised. Add garlic and thyme; cook, stirring, for 1 minute or until fragrant. Stir in stock; cover, bring to the boil. Reduce heat to low; simmer, covered, for 30 minutes. Stir in vinegar; season to taste.

2 Meanwhile, make cheesy sweet potato toasts.

3 Serve soup with cheesy sweet potato toasts and sprinkled with extra thyme leaves, if you like.

cheesy sweet potato toasts Preheat oven to 200°C/400°F. Line an oven tray with baking paper. Place sweet potato on tray; toss with oil, season; roast for 25 minutes or until tender. Preheat grill (broiler) on high. Line a large oven tray with foil. Spread pesto over one side of sweet potato slices. Place sweet potato on foil-lined tray; sprinkle evenly with cheese. Grill for 2 minutes or until cheese is golden and bubbling.

nutritional count per serving 25g total fat (5g saturated fat); 1738kJ (415 cal); 31g carbohydrate; 13g protein; 12g fibre

tips It's important to have a well-flavoured beef stock for this recipe. Make your own or purchase a good-quality stock from a butcher or gourmet deli. You can substitute gruyère with vintage cheddar, if preferred.

do-ahead Soup can be made a day ahead; keep refrigerated. Soup is suitable to freeze for 1 month. Sweet potato can be roasted up to 4 hours ahead; keep refrigerated, then grill with pesto and cheese just before serving.

GREEN CURRY ZOODLE SOUP POTS

PREP + COOK TIME 20 MINUTES (+ STANDING) **SERVES** 4

2 LARGE ZUCCHINI (300G)

200G (6½ OUNCES) DAIKON

⅓ CUP (80ML) FISH SAUCE

¼ CUP (75G) GREEN CURRY PASTE

3 TEASPOONS BROWN SUGAR

400ML COCONUT CREAM

¼ CUP (60ML) LIME JUICE

75G (2½ OUNCES) GREEN BEANS, HALVED LENGTHWAYS

200G (6½ OUNCES) FRIED TOFU PUFFS, CHOPPED COARSELY

½ CUP (75G) ROASTED CASHEWS, CHOPPED

1 CUP LOOSELY PACKED FRESH THAI BASIL LEAVES

4 KAFFIR LIME LEAVES, SHREDDED FINELY

1 LITRE (4 CUPS) BOILING WATER

1 Use a julienne peeler, spiraliser or julienne attachment on a mandoline, or V-slicer to cut zucchini and daikon into long thin strips.

2 Combine fish sauce, curry paste, sugar, coconut cream and lime juice in a medium jug. Divide mixture among four 1-litre (4-cup) heatproof jars with lids.

3 Divide zucchini, daikon, beans and remaining ingredients, except boiling water, in order, among jars.

4 Just before serving, divide boiling water among jars; stir (do not shake). Stand for 5 minutes.

nutritional count per serving 36g total fat (20g saturated fat); 1962kJ (469 cal); 16g carbohydrate; 16g protein; 8g fibre

tip Zoodle (zucchini noodle) pots are great for dinner out-and-about, such as at an open-air cinema or a picnic. Take the jars pre-assembled in a cooler and bring the boiling water separately in a preheated vacuum flask.

do-ahead The jars can be assembled up to 4 hours ahead.

serving suggestion You can add 100g (3 ounces) dried rice vermicelli noodles, prepared following pack directions, to the soups just before serving, for 18.9g carbohydrate per serve.

PROVENÇALE LENTIL & CHILLI SQUID SOUP WITH ROUILLE

PREP + COOK TIME 1 HOUR 10 MINUTES **SERVES** 4

1 CUP (200G) FRENCH-STYLE GREEN LENTILS

1 FRESH LONG RED CHILLI, SEEDED, SLICED THINLY

1 TABLESPOON EXTRA VIRGIN OLIVE OIL

1 LARGE ONION (200G), CHOPPED FINELY

3 CLOVES GARLIC, CRUSHED

3 ANCHOVY FILLETS, CHOPPED FINELY

2 MEDIUM CARROTS (240G), CHOPPED FINELY

2 CELERY STALKS (300G), CHOPPED FINELY

⅓ CUP FIRMLY PACKED FRESH FLAT-LEAF PARSLEY LEAVES, CHOPPED, STALKS RESERVED

3 FRESH THYME SPRIGS

2 BAY LEAVES

6 MEDIUM ZUCCHINI FLOWERS WITH STEMS ATTACHED (120G)

1.5 LITRES (6 CUPS) VEGETABLE STOCK

CHILLI SQUID

500G (1 POUND) SQUID HOODS, CLEANED

1 FRESH LONG RED CHILLI, SEEDED, CHOPPED FINELY

3 CLOVES GARLIC, SLICED THINLY

1 TABLESPOON LEMON RIND STRIPS (SEE TIPS)

1 TABLESPOON EXTRA VIRGIN OLIVE OIL

CHEAT'S ROUILLE

2 TABLESPOONS CHOPPED DRAINED CHAR-GRILLED CAPSICUM (BELL PEPPER) (SEE TIPS)

½ CUP (150G) MAYONNAISE

1 Make chilli squid and cheat's rouille.

2 Place lentils in a large saucepan; cover with water, bring to the boil. Drain. Repeat the process two more times.

3 Place chilli in a small bowl of cold water; refrigerate.

4 Heat the oil in a large saucepan. Cook onion, stirring, for 5 minutes or until soft. Add garlic, anchovy, carrot, celery, chopped parsley stalks, thyme and bay leaves; cook, stirring, for 5 minutes.

5 Tear the petals from the zucchini flowers; reserve petals. Slice the attached zucchini finely. Add zucchini to the pan with drained lentils and stock; bring to the boil. Simmer for 15 minutes or until vegetables are tender, skimming any scum from the top occasionally. Stir in chopped parsley leaves. Season to taste.

6 Meanwhile, cook squid in a heated large frying pan over medium-high heat, in batches, for 1 minute each side. Slice squid thinly. Return squid to the pan with remaining marinade; bring to the boil. Season to taste. Toss through reserved petals and drained chilli.

7 Serve soup topped with chilli squid mixture and rouille.

chilli squid Cut squid in half lengthways. Using a sharp knife, score inside surface in a criss-cross pattern at 5mm (¼-inch) intervals. Place squid in a medium bowl. Add chilli, garlic, rind and oil to bowl; mix well. Cover, refrigerate until required.

cheat's rouille Process ingredients until smooth; season to taste. Cover; refrigerate until required.

nutritional count per serving 43g total fat (6g saturated fat); 2901kJ (693 cal); 35.2g carbohydrate; 37g protein; 12g fibre

tips To create thin strips of lemon rind, use a zester. If you don't have one, peel two long, wide pieces of rind from the lemon, without the white pith, then cut them lengthways into thin strips. We used bottled char-grilled piquillo peppers for the rouille. The lentils are blanched before cooking to give a clear soup.

do-ahead Soup and rouille can be made a day ahead; keep covered, separately, in the fridge. Chilli squid can be refrigerated for 6 hours; it is best cooked close to serving.

HEARTY SPANISH PORK & CHORIZO SOUP

PREP + COOK TIME 2 HOURS 40 MINUTES (+ STANDING) **SERVES** 6

3 ANCHO CHILLIES (30G) (SEE TIPS)

3 GUAJILLO CHILLIES (25G) (SEE TIPS)

1 CUP (250ML) BOILING WATER

¼ CUP (60ML) OLIVE OIL

1.2KG (2½ POUNDS) PORK SCOTCH FILLET, CUT INTO 5CM (2-INCH) CUBES

1 LARGE ONION (200G), CHOPPED FINELY

2 SMOKED CHORIZO (200G), SLICED THINLY

1 MEDIUM RED CAPSICUM (BELL PEPPER) (200G), CHOPPED FINELY

4 CLOVES GARLIC, CHOPPED FINELY

¼ CUP LOOSELY PACKED FRESH MARJORAM LEAVES, CHOPPED FINELY

1 TABLESPOON SMOKED PAPRIKA

¼ TEASPOON GROUND CUMIN

2 RIPE MEDIUM TOMATOES (300G), SEEDED, CHOPPED FINELY

1.5 LITRES (6 CUPS) CHICKEN STOCK

420G (13½ OUNCES) CANNED CANNELLINI BEANS, DRAINED, RINSED

1 SMALL RED ONION (100G), CHOPPED FINELY

1 CUP LOOSELY PACKED FRESH CORIANDER (CILANTRO) LEAVES

1 Toast chillies in a frying pan over high heat for 2 minutes each side or until aromatic and smoky. Remove and discard stems from chillies; place in a medium heatproof bowl. Pour the boiling water over chillies; stand for 20 minutes. Reserve ½ cup of the soaking liquid; drain chillies. Blend or process chillies with reserved liquid until smooth.

2 Heat oil in a flameproof casserole dish or large saucepan over medium heat. Cook pork, in batches, for 6 minutes or until browned. Remove from pan. Cook onion, chorizo, capsicum and garlic in same pan, stirring occasionally, for 5 minutes or until softened. Add marjoram, paprika, cumin and chilli paste; cook, stirring, for 2 minutes or until fragrant. Stir in tomato; return pork to pan.

3 Add stock; bring to the boil. Reduce heat to low; simmer, skimming surface occasionally, for 2 hours or until pork is very tender. Shred meat with two forks. Add beans; simmer for 2 minutes or until heated through. Season to taste.

4 Serve soup topped with red onion and coriander.

nutritional count per serving 22g total fat (5g saturated fat); 2211kJ (528 cal); 22g carbohydrate; 56g protein; 12g fibre

tips Ancho is the name of dried poblano chilli; it has a mild heat and subtle coffee flavour. Guajillo is a dried, large red chilli with medium heat. Both are available from spice stores, gourmet food stores and some delis, or order them online.

do-ahead Stew can be made a day ahead to the end of step 3.

serving suggestion Serve with cauliflower rice or broccoli rice, see page 179.

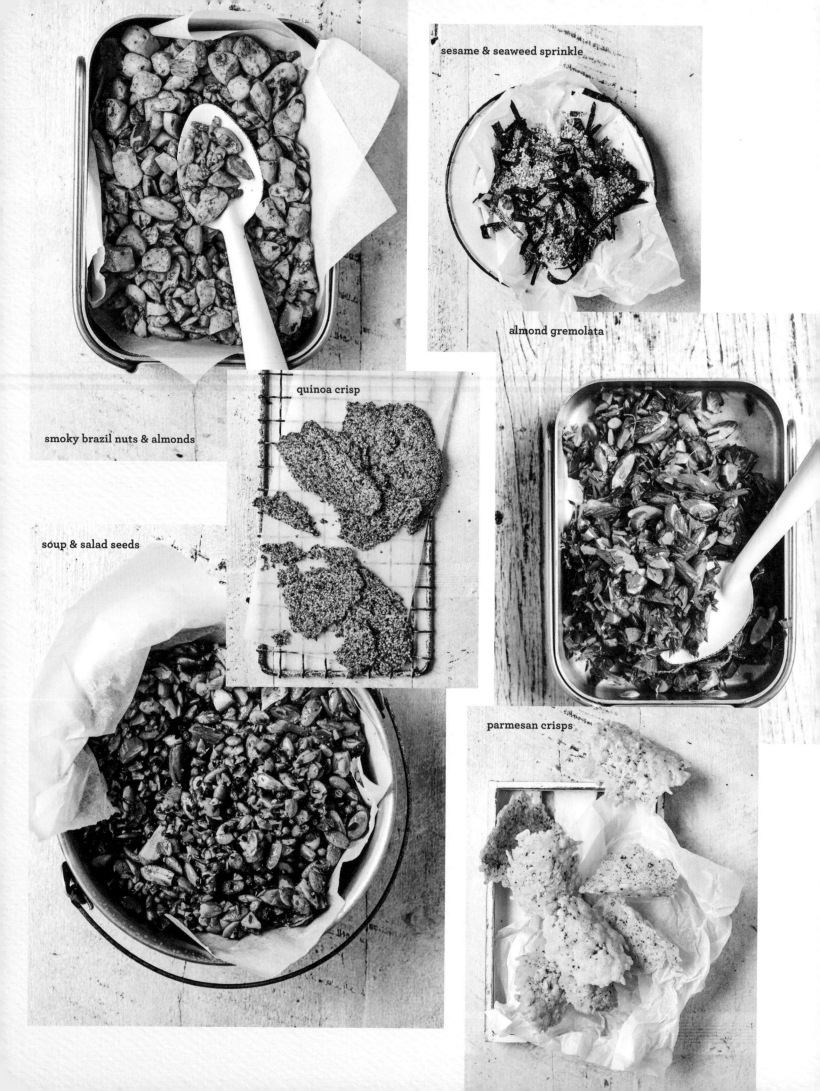

sesame & seaweed sprinkle

almond gremolata

quinoa crisp

smoky brazil nuts & almonds

soup & salad seeds

parmesan crisps

Toppers

Bulk up a soup or stew, while adding a textural layer, with a choice of one of these six toppers.

SMOKY BRAZIL NUTS & ALMONDS

prep + cook time 20 minutes **makes** 1 cup

Preheat oven to 180°C/350°F. Line an oven tray with baking paper. Coarsely chop 1 cup brazil nuts; place on tray with 1 cup blanched almonds and 1 cup rice puffs. Whisk 1 egg white, 2 teaspoons smoked paprika, 1 teaspoon ground cumin and 1 teaspoon sea salt flakes with a fork until combined. Toss spice mixture with nut mixture. Roast for 10 minutes or until golden, stirring halfway through cooking time.

SESAME & SEAWEED SPRINKLE

prep + cook time 15 minutes **makes** 1¼ cups

Using scissors snip 2 nori (seaweed) sheets into fine strips. Place ¼ cup sesame seeds and 1 teaspoon sea salt flakes in a small frying pan; stir constantly over medium heat 5 minutes or until golden. Add nori strips and stir a further 1 minute or until lightly toasted. Transfer to a bowl; stir in ¼ cup fried asian shallots and 1 teaspoon dried chilli flakes.

QUINOA CRISP

prep + cook time 1 hour 30 minutes
makes 2 cups

Preheat oven to 180°C/350°F. Line an oven tray with baking paper. Combine ⅓ cup white quinoa, 2 tablespoons black chia seeds, 2 tablespoons linseeds (flaxseeds), 1 tablespoon extra virgin olive oil and 1 cup water in a small saucepan. Stir over medium heat for 12 minutes until mixture begins to pull away from side of pan and is thick. Add ⅓ cup finely grated parmesan; stir a further 2 minutes. Remove from heat; season. Spread mixture thinly over tray. Cover with a second sheet of baking paper; roll out to 2mm (⅛-in) thick. Bake 20 minutes; remove top paper. Bake a further 20 minutes. Carefully turn crisp over; bake 20 minutes or until golden brown and crisp. Cool. Break into pieces.

ALMOND GREMOLATA

prep + cook time 10 minutes **makes** 1 cup

Coarsely chop ½ cup roasted natural almonds. Heat 30g (1oz) butter in a small saucepan over a medium heat; cook, stirring, until beginning to brown; remove from heat. Add 1 tablespoon finely grated lemon rind and ½ cup chopped fresh flat-leaf parsley.

SOUP & SALAD SEEDS

prep + cook time 10 minutes **makes** ¾ cup

Heat 2 tablespoons olive oil in a small, non-stick frying pan over medium heat. Add ⅓ cup coarsely chopped natural almonds and ¼ cup pepitas (pumpkin seed kernels), cook, stirring, 1 minute. Add 1 tablespoon each of coriander and black sesame seeds; cook, stirring, for a further 2 minutes or until lightly toasted. Cool.

PARMESAN CRISPS

prep + cook time 20 minutes **makes** 6

Preheat oven to 180°C/350°F. Line two oven trays with baking paper. Combine 1 cup finely grated parmesan, 2 teaspoons wholemeal plain (all-purpose) flour, ¼ teaspoon freshly ground black pepper and 1 teaspoon finely chopped fresh rosemary leaves in a medium bowl. Place 12 level tablespoons of mixture onto tray, 5cm (2in) apart; flatten to 8cm (3¼-in) rounds. Bake for 6 minutes or until pale golden. Working quickly, lift using a palette knife; drape over a rolling pin to cool.

BEETROOT, DILL & COCONUT SOUP WITH CRISP GINGER LENTILS

PREP + COOK TIME 45 MINUTES (+ STANDING) **SERVES** 4

½ CUP (125ML) EXTRA VIRGIN OLIVE OIL

2 LARGE BEETROOT (BEETS) (400G), PEELED, GRATED

1 MEDIUM LEEK (350G), SLICED

2 CELERY STALKS (300G), SLICED

3 TEASPOONS GRATED FRESH GINGER

1.5 LITRES (6 CUPS) VEGETABLE STOCK

1 TABLESPOON FRESH LEMON JUICE

½ CUP (125ML) COCONUT MILK

¼ CUP CHOPPED FRESH DILL

400G (12½ OUNCES) CANNED LENTILS, DRAINED, RINSED

1 Heat 2 tablespoons of the oil in a large saucepan over medium heat. Cook beetroot, leek, celery and 2 teaspoons of the ginger, stirring occasionally, for 15 minutes until tender.

2 Add stock, bring to the boil; simmer for 5 minutes. Remove from the heat; stand for 10 minutes. Blend soup, in batches, with lemon juice, ⅓ cup of the coconut milk and 2 tablespoons of the dill until smooth. Return soup to pan; season to taste. Stir occasionally over low heat until hot.

3 Meanwhile, dry lentils well with paper towel. Heat remaining oil in a large frying pan over high heat. Cook lentils and remaining ginger, stirring, for 8 minutes or until crisp like breadcrumbs. Drain on paper towel.

4 Divide soup among serving bowls; drizzle with remaining coconut milk. Top with remaining dill and crisp lentils.

nutritional count per serving 22g total fat (7g saturated fat); 1530kJ (366 cal); 25g carbohydrate; 11g protein; 11g fibre

do-ahead You can make the soup up to 2 days ahead; store in the fridge. Soup can be frozen at the end of step 2 for up to 2 months.

serving suggestion Serve soup with four 40g (1½-ounce) slices seeded rye bread for 14g carbohydrate per serve.

KOREAN BRAISED BEEF RIBS WITH KIMCHI

PREP + COOK TIME 2 HOURS 30 MINUTES **SERVES** 4

1 TABLESPOON VEGETABLE OIL

1KG (2 POUNDS) BEEF SHORT RIBS, CUT 6CM (2½-INCH) HIGH

1 BUNCH GREEN ONIONS (300G)

1 TABLESPOON FINELY CHOPPED FRESH GINGER

2 CLOVES GARLIC, CRUSHED

2 TABLESPOONS SESAME OIL

2 TABLESPOONS RICE WINE VINEGAR

1 TABLESPOON SOY SAUCE

1 TABLESPOON GOCHUJANG (SEE TIPS)

1 LITRE (4 CUPS) WATER

1 CUP (100G) KIMCHI

1 MEDIUM FIRM PEAR (230G), GRATED COARSELY

100G (3 OUNCES) FRESH SHIITAKE MUSHROOMS

1 LARGE DAIKON (800G)

500G (1 POUND) BABY BUK CHOY, QUARTERED LENGTHWAYS

100G (3 OUNCES) ENOKI MUSHROOMS

1 TABLESPOON SESAME SEEDS

½ TEASPOON GOCHUGARU (KOREAN RED PEPPER FLAKES)

1 Heat vegetable oil in a large heavy-based saucepan or flameproof casserole dish over high heat. Season ribs; cook for 8 minutes, turning occasionally, or until browned all over.

2 Chop the white part of the green onions; refrigerate reserved green tops for serving. Add white part of onion, ginger and garlic to pan; cook, stirring, for 30 seconds or until fragrant.

3 Combine sesame oil, rice wine vinegar, soy sauce and gochujang in a large jug. Whisk until combined. Add mixture to pan with the water, kimchi and pear; bring to a simmer. Cook, covered, over low heat, stirring every 30 minutes, for 2 hours or until beef is tender and falls away from the bone; add shiitake mushrooms to pan for last 30 minutes of the cooking time.

4 Meanwhile, use a julienne peeler, spiraliser or julienne attachment on a mandoline, or V-slicer to cut daikon into long thin strips. Add daikon to a large saucepan of boiling salted water; boil for 3 minutes or until just tender. Drain well.

5 Place buk choy and enoki mushroom on top of braised beef rib mixture in pan. Cook, covered, for a further 2 minutes or until vegetables are just tender. Trim the green tops of the onions; cut into long thin strips.

6 Top ribs with green onion; sprinkle with seeds and chilli flakes. Serve with daikon noodles.

nutritional count per serving 41g total fat (11g saturated fat); 2909kJ (695 cal); 16g carbohydrate; 57g protein; 10g fibre

tips Gochujang is a Korean chilli paste, available from Asian food stores. We used mild gochujang paste; you can use hot if preferred. Many Korean rib recipes contain a lot of sugar and mirin, but this version uses a whole pear instead for natural sweetness and added fibre.

do ahead Recipe can be made to the end of step 3 a day ahead.

FRAGRANT VIETNAMESE-STYLE BEEF STEW

PREP + COOK TIME 3 HOURS 10 MINUTES **SERVES** 4

1 TABLESPOON RICE BRAN OIL

1KG (2 POUNDS) BEEF CHUCK STEAK, CUT INTO 3CM (1¼-INCH) CUBES

2 MEDIUM RED ONIONS (340G)

1 STEM FRESH LEMON GRASS, BRUISED, QUARTERED

1 TEASPOON CHINESE FIVE SPICE

3 STAR ANISE

2 WHOLE CLOVES

¼ TEASPOON CARDAMOM SEEDS

5 MEDIUM TOMATOES (750G), CHOPPED

1 LITRE (4 CUPS) WATER

¼ CUP (60ML) FISH SAUCE

2 TABLESPOONS FRESH LIME JUICE

1 TEASPOON SEA SALT FLAKES

2 BUNCHES MIXED HEIRLOOM BABY CARROTS (800G), TRIMMED, PEELED

125G (4 OUNCES) BABY CORN, SLICED DIAGONALLY

1 CUP (80G) BEAN SPROUTS

1 CUP LOOSELY PACKED FRESH THAI BASIL SPRIGS

1 FRESH LONG RED CHILLI, SLICED THINLY

1 MEDIUM LIME (90G), CUT INTO WEDGES

1 Heat oil in a large heavy-based saucepan or flameproof casserole dish over high heat. Cook beef, in two batches, for 5 minutes or until browned all over. Remove from pan.

2 Reduce heat to medium. Chop one of the onions coarsely. Cook chopped onion, stirring, for 5 minutes or until softened. Add lemon grass and spices; cook, stirring, for 1 minute or until fragrant. Stir in tomato; cook, stirring occasionally, for 4 minutes or until soft.

3 Return beef to pan with the water and fish sauce; season with a little freshly ground black pepper. Bring to the boil; reduce heat to low. Simmer, covered, stirring occasionally, for 2 hours or until beef is very tender.

4 Meanwhile, slice remaining onion thinly. Combine sliced onion with lime juice and salt in a medium non-reactive bowl. Stand, covered, for at least 1 hour. Drain before using.

5 Add carrots and corn to beef mixture; simmer, covered, for 20 minutes or until carrots are tender. Season to taste.

6 Top beef stew with bean sprouts, pickled onion, basil sprigs and chilli. Serve with lime wedges.

nutritional count per serving 24g total fat (8g saturated fat); 2381kJ (569 cal); 23g carbohydrate; 59g protein; 14g fibre

tip If you can't find fresh thai basil, use coriander instead.

do-ahead Stew can be made a day ahead and refrigerated; or freeze for up to 2 months. Make pickled onion on day of serving and add the toppings just before serving.

serving suggestion Serve with daikon noodles, see page 172, or broccoli or cauliflower rice, see page 179.

CURRIED LAMB SHANK SOUP

PREP + COOK TIME 3 HOURS 15 MINUTES (+ STANDING) **SERVES** 4

1.5KG (3 POUNDS) LAMB SHANKS

1½ TABLESPOONS GROUND CUMIN

1½ TABLESPOONS GROUND CORIANDER

½ BUNCH FRESH CORIANDER (CILANTRO) (SEE TIP)

2 LARGE ONIONS (400G)

1 TABLESPOON CHOPPED FRESH GINGER

4 CLOVES GARLIC, CHOPPED COARSELY

1 TABLESPOON PEELED CHOPPED FRESH TURMERIC

2 FRESH LONG GREEN CHILLIES, SEEDED, CHOPPED COARSELY

40G (1½ OUNCES) GHEE

1 TABLESPOON FENUGREEK SEEDS

2 TABLESPOONS CURRY LEAVES

500G (1 POUND) RIPE TOMATOES, SEEDED, CHOPPED FINELY

1.5 LITRES (6 CUPS) BEEF STOCK

1 LITRE (4 CUPS) BOILING WATER

1 FRESH LONG GREEN CHILLI, EXTRA, SLICED THINLY

1 Place lamb in a large bowl; rub with cumin and ground coriander. Season well; stand at room temperature for 15 minutes.

2 Meanwhile, separate coriander leaves from stems; refrigerate reserved coriander leaves for serving. Chop stems; you will need 2 tablespoons of stems. Coarsely chop one of the onions; process stems with ginger, garlic, chopped onion, turmeric and chilli in a small processor until a coarse paste forms.

3 Heat half of ghee in a large heavy-based saucepan over medium heat. Cook lamb, in batches, for 5 minutes or until browned all over. Remove from pan. Wipe out pan with paper towel; add remaining ghee. Thinly slice remaining onion. Cook fenugreek seeds and sliced onion over low heat, stirring, for 5 minutes or until softened. Increase heat to medium, add turmeric paste; cook, stirring, for 3 minutes or until fragrant. Add curry leaves and tomato; cook, stirring, for 2 minutes.

4 Stir in stock and the water; return lamb to pan. Bring to the boil; reduce heat to low. Simmer, covered, for 1 hour 45 minutes. Remove lid; cook, uncovered, for a further 45 minutes or until lamb is tender and falling off the bone.

5 Remove shanks from pan. When cool enough to handle, pull meat from shanks in small chunks; discard bones, fat and gristle. Return meat to pan; season soup to taste. Stir soup over medium heat until hot. Serve sprinkled with reserved coriander leaves and extra chilli.

nutritional count per serving 41g total fat (18g saturated fat); 2516kJ (601 cal); 15g carbohydrate; 41g protein; 7g fibre

tip It's important to wash the fresh coriander thoroughly, especially at the base of the stems and roots.

do-ahead Soup can be made up to 3 days ahead or frozen for up to 2 months.

serving suggestion Serve soup with 8 small pappadums (24g) for 15.5g carbohydrate per serve.

mushy peas & mint

sweet potato toasts

broccoli rice

shake & bake wedges

cloud bread buns

cauliflower rice

Accompaniments

These low-carb alternatives are a perfect complement to a hot soup or stew.

SWEET POTATO TOASTS

prep + cook time 40 minutes **serves** 6

Preheat oven to 200°C/400°F. Line an oven tray with baking paper. Cut 3 small orange sweet potatoes (750g) into 1cm (½-in) thick slices lengthways. Place sweet potato on tray; toss with 1 tablespoon olive oil, season. Roast for 25 minutes or until tender. Preheat grill (broiler) on high. Line a large oven tray with foil. Divide ½ cup spinach dip between slices; spread over one side of sweet potatoes. Place on tray; sprinkle with ⅓ cup coarsely grated gruyère. Grill 2 minutes or until golden.

MUSHY PEAS & MINT

prep + cook time 10 minutes **serves** 4

Boil, steam or microwave 500g (1lb) frozen baby green peas until just tender; drain. Blend or process peas, ½ cup firmly packed fresh mint leaves, ½ cup (120g) crème fraîche and 1 teaspoon lemon juice until almost smooth; season to taste. Sprinkle with small mint leaves, if you like

BROCCOLI RICE

prep + cook time 10 minutes **serves** 4

Coarsely chop 750g (1½lbs) broccoli with stems. Process broccoli using pulse button until resembles rice grains. Heat 2 tablespoons olive oil in a wok or large frying pan over medium heat. Add 2 crushed cloves garlic, 2 teaspoons grated fresh ginger (optional) and 1 finely chopped fresh small red chilli; stir for 1 minute or until fragrant. Add chopped broccoli; stir occasionally for 4 minutes or until softened. Season to taste.

SHAKE & BAKE WEDGES

prep + cook time 50 minutes **serves** 4

Preheat oven to 220°C/425°F. Line a large oven tray with baking paper; brush paper with 1 tablespoon olive oil. Cut 2 small orange sweet potatoes (500g) and 2 large parsnips (700g) into wedges, toss with 1 teaspoon each smoked paprika and sea salt flakes. Spread wedges over tray. Repeat with 1 bunch baby beetroot (500g), cut into wedges. Bake for 40 minutes or until tender.

CLOUD BREAD BUNS

prep + cook time 40 minutes **makes** 8

Preheat oven to 140°C/280°F. Line two large oven trays with baking paper. Whisk 3 egg whites and ¼ teaspoon cream of tartar in a medium bowl until firm peaks form. Whisk 3 egg yolks, ¼ cup cottage cheese and ¼ teaspoon salt in a large bowl until combined, fold egg white mixture into cheese mixture. Spoon into eight 9cm (3¾-in) rounds on trays, 10cm (4in) apart. Bake for 30 minutes or until pale golden. Cool on trays.

CAULIFLOWER RICE

prep + cook time 15 minutes **serves** 4

Coarsely chop 750g (1½lbs) cauliflower with stems. Process cauliflower using pulse button until resembles rice grains. Heat 2 tablespoons olive oil in a wok over medium heat. Add 2 crushed cloves garlic and 2 teaspoons finely grated fresh ginger (optional); stir 1 minute or until fragrant. Add chopped cauliflower; stir occasionally for 4 minutes or until softened. Season to taste; sprinkle with chopped fresh flat-leaf parsley.

JERUSALEM ARTICHOKE, APPLE & CAULI SOUP WITH SPROUTS

PREP + COOK TIME 1 HOUR (+ STANDING) **SERVES** 4

60G (2 OUNCES) BUTTER

500G (1 POUND) JERUSALEM ARTICHOKES (SUNCHOKES), PEELED, SLICED

½ SMALL CAULIFLOWER (500G), CHOPPED

2 LARGE RED APPLES (400G), PEELED, CORED, CHOPPED COARSELY

2 CLOVES GARLIC, CHOPPED COARSELY

1 LITRE (4 CUPS) CHICKEN STOCK

1 TABLESPOON LEMON JUICE

¼ CUP (60ML) EXTRA VIRGIN OLIVE OIL

400G (12½ OUNCES) BRUSSELS SPROUTS, TRIMMED, HALVED

⅓ CUP (45G) SKINLESS ROASTED HAZELNUTS, HALVED (SEE TIP)

1 Melt butter in a large saucepan over high heat. Add artichoke; cook, stirring, for 10 minutes or until caramelised and golden. Reduce heat to medium; add cauliflower, apple and garlic. Cook, stirring, for 2 minutes or until softened. Add stock; bring to the boil. Reduce heat to low; simmer, covered, for 25 minutes or until vegetables are tender.
2 Stand mixture for 10 minutes to cool slightly. Add lemon juice. Blend soup, in batches, until smooth. Return to pan; season to taste. Stir occasionally over low heat until hot.
3 Meanwhile, heat 2 tablespoons of the oil in a large frying pan or wok over medium-high heat. Stir-fry sprouts for 4 minutes or until bright green, slightly charred and almost tender.
4 Divide soup among bowls; top evenly with sprouts. Season; serve drizzled with remaining oil and sprinkled with hazelnuts.

nutritional count per serving 35g total fat (11g saturated fat); 2093kJ (500 cal); 29g carbohydrate; 10g protein; 14g fibre
tip To roast hazelnuts, spread on an oven tray; roast in a 180°C/350°F oven for 7 minutes or until nuts are golden brown. Or, place nuts in a heavy-based frying pan, stirring constantly over medium heat until they are evenly browned.
do-ahead Soup can be made up to 1 day ahead, to the end of step 2, or freeze soup for up to 2 months.

ROAST CHICKEN, CELERIAC & BLACK BARLEY SOUP

PREP + COOK TIME 2 HOURS (+ STANDING) **SERVES** 4

⅓ CUP (80ML) EXTRA VIRGIN OLIVE OIL

1 TABLESPOON DRIED OREGANO

1 TABLESPOON SMOKED PAPRIKA

2 TEASPOONS CHILLI FLAKES

1 MEDIUM BULB GARLIC (70G), BROKEN IN HALF

4 CHICKEN MARYLANDS (1.4KG)

1 MEDIUM CELERIAC (CELERY ROOT) (750G),
PEELED, CUT INTO 2CM (¾-INCH) PIECES

½ BUNCH FRESH FLAT-LEAF PARSLEY

1 LARGE ONION (200G), SLICED THINLY

2 STICKS CELERY (300G), TRIMMED, CHOPPED

1 SMALL FENNEL BULB (200G), SLICED THINLY

2.5 LITRES (10 CUPS) SALT-REDUCED
CHICKEN STOCK

½ CUP (100G) BLACK BARLEY, RINSED (SEE TIPS)

1 BUNCH CAVOLO NERO (200G), TRIMMED

½ CUP (40G) FINELY GRATED PARMESAN

1 Preheat oven to 220°C/425°F. Line two large shallow roasting pans with baking paper.

2 Combine half the oil, the oregano, paprika, chilli and garlic in a large bowl; season well. Add chicken and celeriac; mix well to coat evenly. Divide mixture between pans, placing chicken skin-side up. Roast for 40 minutes or until chicken is golden brown

3 Meanwhile, heat remaining oil in a large saucepan over low-medium heat. Coarsely chop parsley stems; you will need ¼ cup. Refrigerate leaves. Cook onion, celery, fennel and parsley stems, stirring, for 10 minutes or until softened. Add chicken and celeriac mixture, including the roasting juices. Squeeze garlic from skins; add to pan. Discard skins.

4 Add stock to the pan; bring to the boil. Stir in barley. Reduce heat to low; simmer, covered with a tight-fitting lid for 40 minutes or until chicken and vegetables are tender. Remove chicken from pan; stand until cool enough to handle. Break chicken into chunks; discard skin and bones. Skim fat from surface of soup. Return chicken to pan with cavolo nero. Simmer for 10 minutes; season to taste.

5 Thinly slice half reserved parsley leaves; stir into soup. Divide soup among bowls; top evenly with parmesan and remaining parsley leaves. Serve.

nutritional count per serving 54g total fat (12g saturated fat); 4053kJ (969 cal); 30g carbohydrate; 50g protein; 19g fibre

tips For less heat, reduce the chilli flakes to 1 teaspoon. Black barley is available from some health food stores, delis and gourmet food stores. You can use pearl barley instead.

do-ahead Stew can be made up to 2 days ahead or freeze for up to 3 months. The barley will thicken the mixture on standing; add a little extra stock or water when reheating.

Grills
&BAKES

MEGA MUSHROOM
CHEESE BURGER

PREP + COOK TIME 50 MINUTES **SERVES** 4

Portobello mushrooms have a moreish savoury taste known as 'umami', are the only vegan sources of vitamin D, and are also a good source of B vitamins.

8 X 100G (3-OUNCE) LARGE PORTOBELLO MUSHROOMS, TRIMMED

½ CUP (125ML) OLIVE OIL

1 MEDIUM EGGPLANT (300G), CUT INTO 4 SLICES CROSSWAYS

200G (6½ OUNCES) GOAT'S FETTA, CUT INTO 4 SLICES CROSSWAYS

400G (12½ OUNCES) TOMATOES, SLICED THICKLY

1 TABLESPOON BALSAMIC VINEGAR

2 SMALL AVOCADOS (400G), SLICED THINLY

100G (3 OUNCES) BABY SPINACH

ROCKET & WALNUT PESTO

50G (1½ OUNCES) BABY ROCKET (ARUGULA) LEAVES

½ CUP FIRMLY PACKED FRESH BASIL LEAVES

½ CUP (50G) WALNUTS

1 CLOVE GARLIC, CRUSHED

2 TABLESPOONS FINELY GRATED PARMESAN

½ CUP (125ML) EXTRA VIRGIN OLIVE OIL

2 TABLESPOONS FRESH LEMON JUICE

1 Preheat oven to 200°C/400°F. Line three oven trays with baking paper.

2 Place mushrooms cup-side up, on two trays. Drizzle with 2 tablespoons of the oil; season. Place eggplant on remaining tray. Drizzle with ¼ cup of the remaining oil. Roast mushrooms and eggplant for 35 minutes.

3 Meanwhile, make rocket and walnut pesto.

4 Place fetta on an oven tray. Place under hot grill (broiler) for 5 minutes or until browned lightly.

5 Toss tomatoes in remaining oil and the vinegar in a medium bowl.

6 Place four mushrooms, cup-side up, on plates. Top with eggplant, tomato, avocado, spinach, fetta, pesto and remaining mushrooms, cup-side down. Season.

rocket & walnut pesto Blend or process rocket, basil, walnuts, garlic and parmesan until combined. Add oil in a thin steady stream, blend until smooth. Add juice; blend until just combined. If pesto is too thick, add 1 tablespoon water. Season to taste. (Makes 1 cup)

nutritional count per serving 99.9g total fat (21.6g saturated fat); 4319kJ (1032 cal); 6.3g carbohydrate; 21.2g protein; 10.8g fibre

tip Store any leftover pesto covered by a thin film of olive oil in the fridge for up to 1 week. Use in sandwiches or swirled through vegetable soups.

do-ahead Pesto can be made a day ahead; keep tightly covered in the fridge. It can also be frozen in a small container for up to 3 months.

MIDDLE EASTERN CARROT SALAD WITH LAMB SKEWERS

PREP + COOK TIME 35 MINUTES (+ REFRIGERATION) **SERVES** 4

You will need 8 metal or bamboo skewers.

¼ CUP (75G) TANDOORI PASTE

½ CUP (140G) GREEK-STYLE YOGHURT

800G (1½ POUNDS) BONELESS LAMB LEG, CUT INTO 3CM (1¼-INCH) CUBES

¼ CUP (20G) SHREDDED COCONUT

1½ TABLESPOONS OLIVE OIL

1 MEDIUM RED ONION (170G), CHOPPED FINELY

½ TEASPOON GROUND CUMIN

2 LARGE CARROTS (360G), CUT INTO RIBBONS

2 TABLESPOONS CURRANTS

½ CUP LOOSELY PACKED FRESH MINT LEAVES, SHREDDED FINELY

1 TABLESPOON LEMON JUICE

1 TEASPOON HONEY

⅓ CUP (95G) GREEK-STYLE YOGHURT, EXTRA

1 MEDIUM LEMON (140G), CUT INTO WEDGES

1 Combine tandoori paste and yoghurt in a small bowl. Thread lamb three-quarters of the way onto skewers. Place skewers in a shallow dish; coat in tandoori mixture. Cover; refrigerate for 1 hour.

2 Meanwhile, heat a medium frying pan over medium-high heat. Cook coconut, stirring, for 1 minute or until lightly golden. Remove from pan.

3 Heat 1 teaspoon of the oil in same pan over medium-high heat. Cook onion, stirring, for 3 minutes or until soft. Cook cumin, stirring, for 1 minute or until fragrant. Transfer mixture to a large heatproof bowl, add carrot, currants and mint; mix well.

4 Whisk remaining oil, juice and honey in a small jug until well combined; season to taste. Drizzle dressing over carrot salad; toss to coat.

5 Cook skewers on a heated oiled grill plate (or grill or barbecue) over medium-high heat for 3 minutes each side or until just cooked through.

6 Toss coconut through salad. Serve skewers with salad, drizzled with extra yoghurt and lemon wedges.

nutritional count per serving 31g total fat (12g saturated fat); 2595kJ (620 cal); 20g carbohydrate; 62g protein; 7g fibre

tips If using metal skewers, oil them before use. Soak bamboo skewers for at least 30 minutes before using to prevent burning when cooking. If you make the carrot salad in advance, reserve the toasted coconut until serving, so it stays crunchy.

WASABI FISH BURGERS
IN CLOUD BREAD BUNS

PREP + COOK TIME 1 HOUR 20 MINUTES (+ COOLING) **SERVES** 4

4 X 200G (6½ OUNCES) SKINLESS FIRM WHITE FISH FILLETS, HALVED (SEE TIPS)

1 TEASPOON SESAME SEEDS

¼ TEASPOON CHILLI FLAKES

1 TABLESPOON VEGETABLE OIL

1 BUNCH BABY BUK CHOY (500G), SLICED THINLY

½ SMALL CARROT (35G), PEELED, CUT INTO LONG THIN MATCHSTICKS

2 GREEN ONIONS (SCALLIONS), SLICED THINLY LENGTHWAYS

¼ TEASPOON SESAME OIL

1 TABLESPOON RICE WINE VINEGAR

1 TABLESPOON LIGHT SOY SAUCE

½ CUP (150G) WHOLE-EGG MAYONNAISE

2 TEASPOONS WASABI PASTE (SEE TIPS)

CLOUD BREAD BUNS

3 EGGS, SEPARATED

¼ TEASPOON CREAM OF TARTAR

¼ CUP (50G) COTTAGE CHEESE

¼ TEASPOON SEA SALT FLAKES

1 TEASPOON SESAME SEEDS

1 Make cloud bread buns.

2 Sprinkle fish with sesame seeds and chilli; season. Heat vegetable oil in a large frying pan over medium heat. Cook fish for 3 minutes each side or until cooked through.

3 Meanwhile, combine buk choy, carrot, green onion, sesame oil, vinegar and soy sauce in a large bowl. Combine mayonnaise and wasabi in a small bowl.

4 Spread flat side of four of the buns with wasabi mayonnaise. Top evenly with buk choy slaw and fish; sandwich with the remaining buns.

cloud bread buns Preheat oven to 140°C/280°F. Line two large oven trays with baking paper. Whisk egg whites and cream of tartar in a medium bowl until firm peaks form. Whisk egg yolks, cottage cheese and salt in a large bowl until well combined. Gently fold egg white mixture through cheese mixture. Spoon mixture into eight 9cm (3¾-inch) rounds on trays, about 10cm (4 inches) apart. Sprinkle with sesame seeds. Bake for 40 minutes or until pale golden. Cool on trays.

nutritional count per serving 43g total fat (7g saturated fat); 2576kJ (616 cal); 4g carbohydrate; 51g protein; 3g fibre

tips You could use any white fish fillet, such as cod, ling or snapper. Use as much or as little wasabi, to taste. You could swap the buk choy for wombok (napa cabbage), if you like. The cloud buns are a great low-carb option for any kind of sandwich. For a sandwich with a sweet filling, such as jam, omit the salt in the buns. For a gluten-free version, use a gluten-free soy sauce.

do-ahead The cloud bread buns are best made on day of serving; store in an airtight container.

BOMBAY ROAST LAMB & VEGETABLES

PREP + COOK TIME 1 HOUR 15 MINUTES (+ STANDING) **SERVES** 4

1 BUNCH BABY (DUTCH) CARROTS (400G), TRIMMED, SCRUBBED

500G (1 POUND) BUTTERNUT PUMPKIN, PEELED, CUT INTO 4CM (1½-INCH) PIECES

2 MEDIUM ONIONS (300G), CUT INTO WEDGES

¼ CUP COARSELY CHOPPED FRESH CORIANDER (CILANTRO) LEAVES

1 TEASPOON GROUND TURMERIC

2 TEASPOONS FINELY GRATED LEMON RIND

2 TABLESPOONS FRESH LEMON JUICE

1 TABLESPOON CUMIN SEEDS

1 TABLESPOON GRATED FRESH GINGER

¼ CUP (60ML) OLIVE OIL

4 X 3-CUTLET FRENCH-TRIMMED LAMB RACKS (540G)

1 CUP (120G) FROZEN PEAS

1 CUP (280G) GREEK-STYLE YOGHURT

2 TABLESPOONS MANGO CHUTNEY

⅓ CUP LOOSELY PACKED FRESH CORIANDER (CILANTRO) LEAVES, EXTRA

1 Preheat oven to 220°C/425°F. Line a large roasting pan with baking paper. Place carrots, pumpkin and onion in pan.

2 Combine coriander, turmeric, lemon rind and juice, cumin seeds, ginger and oil in a small bowl; season. Place lamb in a medium bowl; pour half the turmeric mixture over lamb and the other half over vegetables. Roast vegetables for 15 minutes. Place lamb on top of vegetables; roast for a further 20 minutes for medium or until lamb is cooked to your liking. Stir through peas; roast for a further 1 minute. Rest lamb, covered loosely, for 10 minutes.

3 Meanwhile, combine yoghurt and chutney in a small bowl.

4 Serve roast lamb and vegetables with yoghurt mixture and extra coriander.

nutritional count per serving 27g total fat (7g saturated fat); 2022kJ (483 cal); 30g carbohydrate; 26g protein; 9g fibre

tips You could swap the pumpkin for brussels sprouts, broccoli or cauliflower. Green beans are a lower carb option than peas, if preferred. You could use a store-bought lime pickle instead of mango chutney.

VIETNAMESE-STYLE PORK IN LETTUCE CUPS

PREP + COOK TIME 2 HOURS (+ REFRIGERATION & STANDING) **SERVES** 4

You will need to start this recipe a day ahead.

½ CUP (125ML) FISH SAUCE

½ CUP (125ML) FRESH LIME JUICE

⅓ CUP (75G) CASTER (SUPERFINE) SUGAR

4 CLOVES GARLIC, CHOPPED

4 FRESH LONG RED CHILLIES, CHOPPED

8 GREEN ONIONS (SCALLIONS), CHOPPED

1 BUNCH FRESH CORIANDER (CILANTRO), ROOTS, STEMS AND LEAVES SEPARATED

1.2KG (2½-POUND) PORK SCOTCH FILLET

2 TABLESPOONS VEGETABLE OIL

2 LEBANESE CUCUMBERS (260G)

1 BUTTER (BOSTON) LETTUCE (200G), LEAVES SEPARATED

400G (12½ OUNCES) HEIRLOOM TOMATOES, SLICED THICKLY

2 CUPS (160G) BEAN SPROUTS

1 MEDIUM LIME (90G), CUT INTO CHEEKS

1 Process fish sauce, lime juice, sugar, garlic, chilli, green onion and coriander roots and stems until almost smooth. Place pork in a glass or ceramic dish; rub marinade all over pork. Cover; refrigerate for 6 hours or overnight.

2 Preheat oven to 180°C/350°F.

3 Remove pork from marinade; reserve marinade. Heat oil in a large flameproof roasting pan over medium-high heat. Cook pork until browned all over. Transfer pan to oven. Roast pork for 1½ hours or until cooked through. Remove pork from oven; rest, covered loosely, for 15 minutes.

4 Meanwhile, place reserved marinade in a small saucepan over low heat. Simmer, stirring occasionally, for 15 minutes, or until reduced by half. Cool.

5 Slice pork. Using a vegetable peeler, peel cucumbers into long thin ribbons.

6 Place pork in lettuce cups with tomato, cucumber, bean sprouts and coriander leaves; drizzle with reduced marinade. Serve with lime cheeks.

nutritional count per serving 14g total fat (2g saturated fat); 2254kJ (539 cal); 29g carbohydrate; 70g protein; 8g fibre

tips Iceberg and cos lettuce can also be used in place of butter lettuce. If you don't have a flameproof roasting pan, brown the pork in a large frying pan, then transfer it to a roasting pan to roast.

BARBECUED MARINATED TOFU WITH CHINESE BROCCOLI

PREP + COOK TIME 35 MINUTES (+ REFRIGERATION) **SERVES** 4

½ TEASPOON GROUND CORIANDER

½ TEASPOON GROUND CUMIN

½ BUNCH FRESH CORIANDER (CILANTRO), STEMS AND ROOTS CHOPPED, LEAVES RESERVED

3 CLOVES GARLIC, CRUSHED

2 TABLESPOONS COARSELY CHOPPED FRESH GINGER

¼ CUP (60ML) VEGETABLE OIL

600G (1¼ POUNDS) FIRM TOFU, SLICED THICKLY

500G (1 POUND) GAI LAN (CHINESE BROCCOLI), TRIMMED, HALVED

2 TABLESPOONS WATER

200G (6½ OUNCES) SNOW PEAS, TRIMMED

2 TABLESPOONS CHINESE BLACK VINEGAR

2 TEASPOONS FISH SAUCE

1 TEASPOON BROWN SUGAR

1 TEASPOON SESAME OIL

1 TEASPOON ASIAN CHILLI OIL

1 FRESH LONG RED CHILLI, SLICED THINLY

2 GREEN ONIONS (SCALLIONS), SLICED THINLY

1 Combine ground spices, 2 tablespoons of coriander roots and stems, garlic, ginger and 1 tablespoon of the oil in a medium bowl. Reserve 1 tablespoon of the marinade.

2 Pat tofu dry. Place tofu in a single layer in a flat ceramic or glass dish. Gently brush marinade on both sides of tofu. Cover; refrigerate for 30 minutes.

3 Heat 1 tablespoon of the oil in a large frying pan or grill plate over medium-high heat. Cook tofu for 2 minutes each side or until tofu is starting to crisp and is heated through. Transfer tofu to a plate; cover to keep warm.

4 Heat remaining oil in a wok or large frying pan over medium-high heat. Stir-fry gai lan stems for 1 minute. Add reserved marinade; stir-fry for 1 minute. Add the water, gai lan leaves, snow peas, vinegar, fish sauce and sugar; stir-fry for 1 minute or until combined and vegetables are tender. Remove from heat; stir in combined sesame and chilli oils.

5 Serve tofu with vegetables, drizzled with pan juices. Top with coriander leaves, fresh chilli and green onion.

nutritional count per serving 31g total fat (4g saturated fat); 1721kJ (411 cal); 11g carbohydrate; 22g protein; 12g fibre

tips For a vegetarian option, use soy sauce instead of fish sauce. You can use your favourite Asian greens in this recipe.

SLOW-COOKED LAMB SHOULDER WITH SMOKY EGGPLANT SALAD

PREP + COOK TIME 4 HOURS (+ REFRIGERATION & STANDING) **SERVES** 6

You will need to start this recipe a day ahead.

1 TABLESPOON CORIANDER SEEDS

1 TABLESPOON CUMIN SEEDS

2 TABLESPOONS EXTRA VIRGIN OLIVE OIL

1 TABLESPOON SMOKED PAPRIKA

2KG (4-POUND) LAMB SHOULDER, BONE-IN

1 MEDIUM BULB GARLIC (70G), PEELED

2 TABLESPOONS POMEGRANATE SEEDS

2 TABLESPOONS POMEGRANATE MOLASSES

1½ CUPS (420G) GREEK-STYLE YOGHURT

1 CUP LOOSELY PACKED FRESH MINT LEAVES

SMOKY EGGPLANT SALAD

4 SMALL EGGPLANTS (920G)

1 TABLESPOON RED WINE VINEGAR

¼ CUP (60ML) EXTRA VIRGIN OLIVE OIL

400G (12½ OUNCES) SPRING ONIONS, SLICED THINLY

2 CUPS (80G) FIRMLY PACKED TRIMMED WATERCRESS

1 Pound seeds using a mortar and pestle until lightly crushed. Combine oil, paprika and crushed seeds in a small bowl; mix well.

2 Place lamb and garlic in a large glass or ceramic dish. Rub spice mixture all over lamb. Cover, refrigerate for 6 hours or overnight.

3 Preheat oven to 160°C/325°F. Place lamb, garlic and any remaining spice mixture in a baking dish. Cover with a sheet of baking paper, then cover tightly with two layers of foil. Bake lamb for 3 hours.

4 Increase the oven to 180°C/350°F. Remove foil and baking paper from dish. Roast lamb for a further 45 minutes or until browned and lamb is falling off the bone. Rest, covered loosely, for 30 minutes. Shred lamb into large chunks; toss garlic through shredded lamb.

5 Meanwhile, make smoky eggplant salad.

6 Serve smoky eggplant salad with lamb and pomegranate seeds. Drizzle with molasses; top with yoghurt and mint.

smoky eggplant salad Pierce eggplants all over with a fork or skewer. Place eggplants directly over a gas flame on a cooktop or barbecue. (You can cover eggplants with an upturned metal bowl to cook the eggplants more quickly.) Cook, turning occasionally, for 18 minutes or until eggplants have started to collapse and the skin is charred and blistered. Transfer to a medium bowl; cool 10 minutes. Remove eggplant stalks and skin; shred lengthways into long pieces. Return eggplant flesh to the bowl with any resting juices. Stir in vinegar; season to taste. Meanwhile, heat oil in a large frying pan over low heat. Cook onion, stirring occasionally, for 20 minutes or until deep golden. Drain onion on paper towel. Just before serving, layer eggplant, watercress and onion on a platter.

nutritional count per serving 35g total fat (12g saturated fat); 2624kJ (627 cal); 21g carbohydrate; 52g protein; 8g fibre

tip If you don't have a gas cooktop or barbecue, roast the eggplants in the oven at 220°C/425°F for 45 minutes or until the eggplants start to collapse.

ONE-PAN FISH ARRABBIATA

PREP + COOK TIME 30 MINUTES **SERVES** 4

2 TABLESPOONS EXTRA VIRGIN OLIVE OIL

2 LARGE RED ONIONS (600G), UNPEELED,
CUT INTO 3CM (1¼-INCH) THICK WEDGES

½ MEDIUM BULB GARLIC (30G) (SEE TIPS)

2 FRESH LONG RED CHILLIES (20G),
SLICED THINLY

4 X 200G (6½ OUNCES) FIRM WHITE
FISH CUTLETS (SEE TIPS)

500G (1 POUND) CHERRY TRUSS TOMATOES

30G (1 OUNCE) BUTTER

½ CUP (10G) LOOSELY PACKED FRESH
BASIL LEAVES

1 Preheat oven to 200°C/400°F.

2 Heat oil in a large flameproof roasting pan over medium heat. Cook onion, stirring, for 3 minutes or until it starts to soften. Add garlic and chilli; cook, stirring, for 2 minutes.

3 Push onion mixture to one side of pan. Add fish; cook for 1 minute each side or until golden. Add tomatoes and butter to pan; season fish and tomatoes. Transfer to oven; bake for 8 minutes or until fish is just cooked through.

4 Serve fish and vegetables sprinkled with basil.

nutritional count per serving 20g total fat (6g saturated fat); 1698kJ (406 cal); 10g carbohydrate; 44g protein; 7g fibre

tips We used half a garlic bulb here, but using whole peeled cloves will still taste great. We used snapper in this recipe, but any white fish cutlet, such as blue eye trevalla or dhufish would also work well.

serving suggestion Serve with a green salad or steamed green vegetables.

BARBECUED MISO CHICKEN WITH CITRUS SALAD

PREP + COOK TIME 1 HOUR 10 MINUTES (+ REFRIGERATION) **SERVES** 4

¼ CUP (60G) WHITE (SHIRO) MISO

⅓ CUP (80ML) EXTRA VIRGIN OLIVE OIL

1 TABLESPOON GRATED FRESH GINGER

2 TABLESPOONS FRESH LEMON JUICE

4 CHICKEN MARYLANDS (1.4KG)

1 LARGE FENNEL BULB (550G), SLICED THINLY, FRONDS RESERVED

2 CELERY STALKS (300G), SLICED THINLY

2 PINK GRAPEFRUIT (700G), PEELED, SEGMENTED (SEE TIPS)

2 MEDIUM ORANGES (480G), PEELED, SEGMENTED (SEE TIPS)

½ CUP (80G) SMOKED ALMONDS, CHOPPED

1 Whisk together miso, 1 tablespoon of the oil, ginger and lemon juice in a large bowl; season with freshly ground black pepper. Add chicken; turn to coat in marinade. Cover; refrigerate for 2 hours or overnight.

2 Heat a covered barbecue to 220°C/425°F. Cook the chicken on barbecue grill over high heat until browned on both sides. Turn burners off underneath chicken, leaving outside burners on. Place chicken on a rack over a roasting pan; cook in covered barbecue by indirect heat for 35 minutes or until cooked through.

3 Combine fennel and remaining oil in a medium bowl; season. Add celery, grapefruit and orange segments and reserved fennel fronds.

4 Serve citrus salad with barbecued chicken; top with almonds.

nutritional count per serving 77g total fat (18g saturated fat); 4088kJ (977 cal); 21g carbohydrate; 46g protein; 9g fibre

tips To segment grapefruit and oranges, peel rind thickly so no white pith remains. Cut between membranes, over a bowl to catch any juice, releasing segments. You can also cook the chicken pieces in a preheated 220°C/425°F oven. Place the chicken pieces on an oven tray; roast for 40 minutes or until cooked through.

serving suggestion Serve with steamed beans, broccolini or asparagus.

WINTER VEGETABLE BAKE
WITH TAHINI SEED CRUMBLE

PREP + COOK TIME 1 HOUR 45 MINUTES **SERVES** 4

1 TABLESPOON EXTRA VIRGIN OLIVE OIL

1 MEDIUM LEEK (350G), TRIMMED, WHITE PART CHOPPED

1 TEASPOON FINELY CHOPPED FRESH ROSEMARY LEAVES

1 TEASPOON FRESH THYME LEAVES

400G (12½ OUNCES) CANNED DICED TOMATOES

1 CUP (250ML) VEGETABLE STOCK

6 CLOVES SMOKED GARLIC, PEELED, BRUISED (SEE TIPS)

2 MEDIUM CARROTS (240G), CUT INTO 2CM (1-INCH) PIECES

3 MEDIUM PARSNIPS (750G), CUT INTO 2CM (1-INCH) PIECES

½ MEDIUM CELERIAC (CELERY ROOT) (375G), CUT INTO 2CM (1-INCH) PIECES

400G (12½ OUNCES) BUTTERNUT PUMPKIN, CUT INTO 2 CM (1-INCH) PIECES

2 CELERY STALKS (300G), SLICED THICKLY

½ CUP (120G) LIGHT SOUR CREAM

SEED TOPPING

¾ CUP (115G) SUNFLOWER SEEDS

½ CUP (60G) ALMOND MEAL

2 TABLESPOONS TAHINI

½ CUP (30G) CHOPPED FRESH FLAT-LEAF PARSLEY

1 Preheat oven to 200°C/400°F.

2 Heat oil in a frying pan over a medium heat; cook leek and herbs, stirring, for 5 minutes or until golden. Add tomatoes, stock and garlic. Simmer for 10 minutes; season to taste.

3 Combine carrot, parsnip, celeriac, pumpkin and celery in a 21cm x 30cm (8½-inch x 12-inch) roasting pan; season. Pour tomato sauce over vegetables; cover with a sheet of baking paper. Cover dish tightly with foil. Bake for 1 hour.

4 Meanwhile, make seed topping.

5 Sprinkle seed topping over vegetable mixture in pan. Bake for a further 15 minutes.

6 Serve vegetable bake topped with dollops of sour cream. Sprinkle with flat-leaf parsley leaves and freshly ground black pepper, if you like.

seed topping Combine all ingredients in a medium bowl.

nutritional count per serving 42g total fat (7g saturated fat); 2754kJ (658 cal); 35g carbohydrate; 23g protein; 24g fibre

tips If you can't find smoked garlic you can use regular garlic, then add a little smoked salt or smoked paprika to the dish. The vegetable bake could also be topped with grated cheese or crumbled goat's cheese.

EGGPLANT & TOMATO BAKES WITH CHEESY YOGHURT TOPPING

PREP + COOK TIME 1 HOUR **SERVES** 4

2 MEDIUM EGGPLANTS (600G), CHOPPED

1 TEASPOON FINE SEA SALT

⅓ CUP (80ML) OLIVE OIL

1 MEDIUM ONION (150G), CHOPPED FINELY

200G (6½ OUNCES) SWISS BROWN MUSHROOMS, SLICED

2 CLOVES GARLIC, CHOPPED FINELY

6 LARGE ROMA (PLUM) TOMATOES (540G), CHOPPED

⅓ CUP COARSELY CHOPPED FRESH FLAT-LEAF PARSLEY

4 EGG YOLKS

2 EGGS

1½ CUPS (420G) GREEK-STYLE YOGHURT

1½ CUPS (120G) FINELY GRATED PARMESAN

1 Preheat oven to 200°C/400°F. Place four 2-cup (500ml) shallow ovenproof dishes on an oven tray.

2 Mix the eggplant with the salt in a colander over a bowl. Stand for 20 minutes.

3 Meanwhile, heat 1 tablespoon of the oil in a large frying pan over a medium heat. Cook the onion, stirring, for 2 minutes or until lightly golden. Cook the mushrooms, stirring, for a further 5 minutes or until browned lightly. Add the garlic and tomato; simmer for 10 minutes.

4 Pat eggplant dry between sheets of paper towel to remove any excess moisture. Heat half of the remaining oil in a large clean frying pan over a high heat; cook half the eggplant, stirring, for 3 minutes or until golden and tender. Repeat with remaining oil and eggplant. Stir eggplant and ¼ cup of the parsley into tomato mixture; season to taste. Spoon the eggplant mixture into the dishes.

5 Combine the egg yolks, whole eggs, yoghurt and 1⅓ cups of the parmesan in a medium bowl. Spoon the yoghurt mixture over the eggplant mixture in dishes; top with remaining parmesan. Bake for 12 minutes or until golden. Sprinkle with remaining parsley.

nutritional count per serving 43g total fat (14g saturated fat); 2445kJ (584 cal); 18g carbohydrate; 28g protein; 6g fibre
do-ahead Eggplant mixture can be made a day ahead, to the end of step 4.
serving suggestion Serve with green leafy salad.

RAINBOW STEAK PLATTER WITH MISO DRESSING

PREP + COOK TIME 45 MINUTES **SERVES** 4

¼ CUP (50G) TRI-COLOURED QUINOA, RINSED

¾ CUP (180ML) WATER

2 TEASPOONS EXTRA VIRGIN OLIVE OIL

2 X 250G (8-OUNCE) RIB-EYE STEAKS

340G (11 OUNCES) ASPARAGUS, HALVED LENGTHWAYS

50G (1½ OUNCES) MIXED SALAD LEAVES

1 MEDIUM BEETROOT (BEET) (175G), PEELED, CUT INTO MATCHSTICKS

2 CUPS (160G) SHREDDED RED CABBAGE

1 LARGE CARROT (180G), CUT INTO MATCHSTICKS

1 MEDIUM AVOCADO (250G), SLICED

2 TABLESPOONS ROASTED CASHEWS

MISO DRESSING

¼ CUP (60G) WHITE (SHIRO) MISO

2 TABLESPOONS ALMOND BUTTER

¼ CUP (60ML) EXTRA VIRGIN OLIVE OIL

1½ TABLESPOONS WATER

1½ TABLESPOONS MIRIN

½ TEASPOON SESAME OIL

1 Place quinoa in a small saucepan with the water; bring to the boil. Reduce heat to low; simmer, covered, for 10 minutes. Remove pan from heat; stand, covered, for a further 5 minutes.

2 Make miso dressing.

3 Heat a grill plate (or barbecue) over high heat. Rub oil into steaks; cook for 3 minutes on each side for medium-rare or until cooked to your liking. Transfer to a plate; season. Rest, covered loosely, for 5 minutes.

4 Meanwhile, pour boiling water over asparagus in a medium heatproof bowl; stand for 1 minute, drain. Refresh under cold running water; drain well.

5 Place salad leaves on a large platter or board. Arrange quinoa, asparagus, beetroot, cabbage, carrot and avocado over salad leaves. Thinly slice steak; add to platter. Drizzle with dressing; sprinkle with cashews. Serve.

miso dressing Stir ingredients in a medium jug until smooth.

nutritional count per serving 43g total fat (8g saturated fat); 2793kJ (667 cal); 23g carbohydrate; 41g protein; 10g fibre

do-ahead Miso dressing can be made up to 2 days ahead; keep refrigerated.

FISH FINGERS
WITH MUSHY BROAD BEANS

PREP + COOK TIME 40 MINUTES (+ REFRIGERATION) **SERVES** 4

¾ CUP (90G) ALMOND MEAL

2 TEASPOONS GARLIC POWDER

2 TABLESPOONS SESAME SEEDS, TOASTED

800G (1½ POUNDS) SKINLESS FIRM WHITE FISH
FILLETS, CUT INTO 1.5CM (¾-INCH) FINGERS

¼ CUP (60ML) EXTRA VIRGIN OLIVE OIL

1 TABLESPOON FRESH LEMON JUICE

2 TEASPOONS DIJON MUSTARD

4 CUPS (160G) FIRMLY PACKED TRIMMED
WATERCRESS

1 SMALL RED ONION (100G), SLICED THINLY

1 MEDIUM LEMON (140G), CUT INTO WEDGES

MUSHY BROAD BEANS

500G (1 POUND) FROZEN BROAD BEANS
(FAVA BEANS)

½ CUP (10G) FIRMLY PACKED FRESH MINT LEAVES,
FIRMLY PACKED

½ CUP (120G) LIGHT SOUR CREAM

¼ TEASPOON GROUND WHITE PEPPER

1 TEASPOON FRESH LEMON JUICE

1 Combine almond meal, garlic powder and sesame seeds in a shallow dish; season. Dip fish, one piece at a time, pressing firmly in almond mixture to coat. Place on a tray; refrigerate for 30 minutes.

2 Meanwhile, make mushy broad beans.

3 Heat 1 tablespoon of the oil in a large frying pan; cook fish fingers for 2 minutes each side or until browned and just cooked through.

4 To make dressing, combine remaining oil, juice and mustard in a screw-top jar; season, shake well. Place watercress and onion in a medium bowl with dressing; toss to combine.

5 Serve fish fingers with watercress salad, mushy broad beans and lemon wedges.

mushy broad beans Boil, steam or microwave broad beans until just tender; drain. Peel broads beans. Blend or process peeled broad beans with remaining ingredients until almost smooth; season to taste.

nutritional count per serving 43g total fat (9g saturated fat); 2863kJ (684 cal); 9g carbohydrate; 58g protein; 15g fibre

tip We used blue-eye trevalla in this recipe, but any white fish fillet will be fine.

do-ahead Fish can be coated up to 6 hours ahead; keep covered in the fridge. Dressing can be made up to a week ahead; keep in a jar in the fridge.

GRILLED MUSSELS
WITH CHICKPEA CRUMBS

PREP + COOK TIME 25 MINUTES **SERVES** 2

⅔ CUP (125G) CANNED CHICKPEAS, RINSED

¼ CUP (30G) ALMOND MEAL

3 CLOVES GARLIC, CRUSHED

¼ CUP FINELY CHOPPED FRESH FLAT-LEAF PARSLEY

1 TEASPOON FINELY GRATED LEMON RIND

2 TABLESPOONS EXTRA VIRGIN OLIVE OIL

1KG (2 POUNDS) CLEANED BLACK MUSSELS (SEE TIPS)

1 MEDIUM LEMON (140G), RIND REMOVED IN THIN STRIPS

FENNEL SALAD

1 MEDIUM FENNEL (300G), SHAVED

1 TRIMMED CELERY STALK (100G), SLICED THINLY ON THE DIAGONAL

1 CUP LOOSELY PACKED FRESH FLAT-LEAF PARSLEY LEAVES

1 TABLESPOON FRESH LEMON JUICE

2 TEASPOONS EXTRA VIRGIN OLIVE OIL

1 Pat chickpeas dry with paper towel. Coarsely mash chickpeas in a medium bowl with a fork. Add almond meal, garlic, parsley, rind and oil; season to taste.

2 Make fennel salad.

3 Preheat grill (broiler) on high heat. Line a large oven tray with foil.

4 Spread mussels in an even layer over tray. Place tray in centre of oven. Grill for 4 minutes or until mussels are beginning to open. Discard top shell of mussels. Divide chickpea mixture among mussels. Grill for a further 3 minutes or until chickpea mixture is golden.

5 Serve mussels with fennel salad, sprinkled with lemon rind.

fennel salad Combine all ingredients in a large bowl; season to taste.

nutritional count per serving 48g total fat (7g saturated fat); 4027kJ (962 cal); 39g carbohydrate; 87g protein; 10g fibre

tips Cleaned mussels are available in bags from some fishmongers and supermarkets. If unavailable, scrub mussels well and remove the beards. Try to use small young parsley leaves for the salad – they are sweeter than larger, older leaves. Serve with lemon wedges, if you prefer.

do-ahead Chickpea mixture can be made a day ahead; keep in the fridge.

GRILLED CHICKEN SKEWERS WITH TURMERIC PESTO & PICKLED ENOKI

PREP + COOK TIME 35 MINUTES (+ STANDING) **SERVES** 4

You will need 12 skewers for this recipe.

200G (6½ OUNCES) ENOKI MUSHROOMS

⅔ CUP (160ML) RICE WINE VINEGAR

¼ CUP (60G) RICE MALT SYRUP

½ CUP (125ML) WATER

2 TEASPOONS YELLOW MUSTARD SEEDS

12 CHICKEN TENDERLOINS (900G)

170G (5½ OUNCES) ASPARAGUS, HALVED LENGTHWAYS

1 TABLESPOON EXTRA VIRGIN OLIVE OIL

60G (2 OUNCES) BABY SPINACH LEAVES

1 MEDIUM LIME (90G), HALVED

TURMERIC PESTO

½ CUP (50G) GRATED FRESH TURMERIC

¼ CUP (40G) ROASTED SALTED CASHEWS

60G (2 OUNCES) PANEER, CRUMBLED (SEE TIPS)

1½ TABLESPOONS LIME JUICE

2 TABLESPOONS EXTRA VIRGIN OLIVE OIL

¼ CUP (60ML) BOILING WATER

½ TEASPOON CHILLI FLAKES

1 Trim base of enoki; place in a non-reactive heatproof bowl. Combine vinegar, syrup, the water and seeds in a small saucepan; bring to the boil. Pour mixture over mushrooms; cool.

2 Meanwhile, heat a grill plate (or barbecue) over medium-high heat. Thread chicken onto skewers. Brush chicken and asparagus with oil; season well. Cook chicken, in batches, for 3 minutes each side or until browned and cooked through. Cook asparagus for 1 minute each side or until lightly charred.

3 Make turmeric pesto.

4 Arrange skewers, asparagus and spinach on a platter; top with turmeric pesto, season to taste. Serve with pickled enoki and lime halves.

turmeric pesto Pulse ingredients in a small food processor until a paste forms. Season to taste.

nutritional count per serving 34g total fat (7g saturated fat); 2721kJ (650 cal); 26g carbohydrate; 55g protein; 4g fibre

tips Paneer is an Indian cheese; it is available from large supermarkets, delis and Indian food stores. If unavailable, use a firm fetta. Soak bamboo skewers in water for 15 minutes before using or oil metal skewers before using.

do-ahead Turmeric pesto can be made a day ahead. It will thicken on standing, so reserve the boiling water to add just before serving.

BEEF WITH CREAMED LEEK & ARTICHOKES

PREP + COOK TIME 30 MINUTES (+ STANDING) **SERVES** 4

30G (1 OUNCE) BUTTER

2 MEDIUM LEEKS (700G), CHOPPED

400G (12½ OUNCES) CANNED CANNELLINI BEANS, DRAINED, RINSED

2 SMALL ZUCCHINI (180G), CUT INTO LONG THIN MATCHSTICKS

½ CUP (125ML) POURING CREAM

4 DRAINED MARINATED ARTICHOKE HEARTS (220G), QUARTERED LENGTHWAYS

2 TEASPOONS LEMON JUICE

2 TABLESPOONS FINELY CHOPPED FRESH FLAT-LEAF PARSLEY

4 X 200G (6½-OUNCE) BEEF SCOTCH FILLET STEAKS

2 TEASPOONS EXTRA VIRGIN OLIVE OIL

160G (5 OUNCES) BABY ROCKET LEAVES

2 TABLESPOONS FLAT-LEAF PARSLEY LEAVES

1 MEDIUM LEMON (140G), CUT INTO CHEEKS

1 Melt butter in a large frying pan over medium heat; cook leek, stirring, for 10 minutes or until soft but not coloured. Add beans and zucchini; cook, stirring, for 2 minutes. Add cream; simmer for 5 minutes. Stir in artichokes, lemon juice and parsley; season to taste.

2 Meanwhile, heat a grill plate (or barbecue) over medium-high heat. Brush steaks with oil; season well. Cook steaks for 2 minutes each side for medium-rare or until cooked to your liking. Transfer steaks to a plate. Rest, covered loosely, for 5 minutes.

3 Slice steaks; serve with creamed leek mixture, rocket and lemon cheeks, sprinkled with parsley.

nutritional count per serving 40g total fat (20g saturated fat); 2886kJ (690 cal); 19g carbohydrate; 54g protein; 16g fibre

tips Instead of scotch fillets, you can use eye fillet, sirloin, t-bone or rump steak, if preferred. It would also be delicious with chicken breast fillets.

BARBECUED FISH WITH BARBECUED SNOW PEA & ASPARAGUS SALAD

PREP + COOK TIME 40 MINUTES (+ COOLING & STANDING) **SERVES** 4

500G (1 POUND) FROZEN BROAD BEANS
(FAVA BEANS)

300G (9½ OUNCES) SNOW PEAS, TRIMMED

340G (11 OUNCES) ASPARAGUS, TRIMMED,
HALVED ON THE DIAGONAL

¼ CUP (60ML) EXTRA VIRGIN OLIVE OIL

4 X 200G (6½-OUNCE) FIRM WHITE FISH FILLETS,
SKIN ON

1 TABLESPOON FRESH LEMON JUICE

1 CUP LOOSELY PACKED FRESH MINT LEAVES

½ CUP (40G) FLAKED ALMONDS, ROASTED
(SEE TIPS)

MINT & LEMON DRESSING

1 CUP LOOSELY PACKED FRESH MINT LEAVES

1 SMALL CLOVE GARLIC, CRUSHED

½ TEASPOON FINELY GRATED LEMON RIND

2 TABLESPOONS FRESH LEMON JUICE

¼ CUP (60ML) EXTRA VIRGIN OLIVE OIL

2 TABLESPOONS WATER

1 Make mint and lemon dressing.

2 Pour boiling water over broad beans in a medium heatproof bowl; stand for 1 minute, drain. Peel broad beans.

3 Preheat barbecue (or grill plate) over high heat.

4 Combine snow peas, asparagus and 1 tablespoon of the oil in a large bowl; season. Coat fish with remaining oil in a shallow dish; season.

5 Barbecue fish, skin-side down, for 3 minutes. Turn, cook for a further 2 minutes or until just cooked through. Transfer fish to a plate; drizzle with lemon juice. Cover loosely to keep warm.

6 Barbecue snow peas and asparagus for 4 minutes, turning once during cooking, or until slightly charred. Transfer to a medium bowl; cool slightly. Stir in broad beans, mint, almonds and dressing.

7 Serve fish with salad.

mint and lemon dressing Blend or process ingredients until smooth; season to taste.

nutritional count per serving 41g total fat (6g saturated fat); 2715kJ (649 cal); 8g carbohydrate; 55g protein; 14g fibre

tips We used snapper in this recipe, but any white fish fillet will be fine. Roasting nuts brings out the flavour. Place nuts in a heavy-based frying pan; stir nuts constantly over medium to high heat until they are evenly browned. You can toast the almonds in a small frying pan on the barbecue. You may need to barbecue the snow peas on the flat plate of the barbecue.

ROAST CAULIFLOWER WITH NUTS & CRÈME FRAÎCHE DRESSING

PREP + COOK TIME 1 HOUR **SERVES** 4

¼ CUP (60ML) EXTRA VIRGIN OLIVE OIL

2 TEASPOONS FINELY GRATED ORANGE RIND

2 TEASPOONS FRESH LEMON THYME LEAVES

2 MEDIUM CAULIFLOWERS (3KG), TRIMMED

¼ CUP (35G) COARSELY CHOPPED HAZELNUTS

¼ CUP (40G) COARSELY CHOPPED BRAZIL NUTS

2 CUPS (80G) FIRMLY PACKED TRIMMED WATERCRESS

½ CUP LOOSELY PACKED FRESH DILL

CRÈME FRAÎCHE DRESSING

150G (4½ OUNCES) SOFT GOAT'S CHEESE

125G (4 OUNCES) CRÈME FRAÎCHE

2 TEASPOONS MILK

1 TEASPOON FRESH LEMON THYME LEAVES

½ TEASPOON FINELY GRATED ORANGE RIND

1 Preheat oven to 220°C/425°F. Line two large oven trays with baking paper.

2 Combine oil, rind and thyme in a small jug; season. Rub cauliflower with 2 tablespoons of the oil mixture. Add nuts to remaining oil mixture; stir to coat.

3 Place cauliflower on one tray and nuts on remaining tray; season. Roast nuts for 4 minutes or until golden and cauliflower for 50 minutes or until just tender and lightly browned.

4 Meanwhile, make crème fraîche dressing.

5 Combine watercress and dill; serve with cauliflower. Sprinkle with roasted nuts and drizzle with crème fraîche dressing

crème fraîche dressing Blend or process all ingredients until smooth; season to taste. Thin with a little extra milk if needed.

nutritional count per serving 49g total fat (18g saturated fat); 2533kJ (605 cal); 11.3g carbohydrate; 22g protein; 15.3g fibre

do-ahead Recipe can be prepared 2 hours ahead, to the end of step 3. Keep covered in the fridge.

beetroot compote

romesco

russian sauce

hazelnut skordalia

caramelised red onions

green hummus

Sauces & topping

Top a grilled steak or any meat of your choice with one of these flavoursome sauces.

HAZELNUT SKORDALIA

prep time 10 minutes **makes** 1½ cups

Process ½ cup skinless roasted hazelnuts, 2 cloves crushed garlic and 70g (2½oz) crustless ciabatta bread until fine crumbs. Add 1½ tablespoons lemon juice, 2 teaspoons white wine vinegar, ¼ cup extra virgin olive oil and ⅔ cup water; process until combined. Stir in 1 tablespoon finely chopped fresh flat-leaf parsley. Season to taste. Serve topped with extra hazelnuts.

goes well with chargrilled eggplant, seafood and chicken.

BEETROOT COMPOTE

prep time 10 minutes **makes** 1⅔ cups

Heat 1 tablespoon olive oil in a medium saucepan over medium heat. Cook 1 small coarsely grated red onion (100g) and 1 tablespoon finely chopped fresh rosemary for 2 minutes or until liquid evaporates. Add 2 peeled, coarsely grated medium beetroot (beets) (350g) and ¾ cup water. Cook, covered, stirring occasionally for 10 minutes or until tender; stir in ½ cup vincotto. Cook, uncovered, stirring occasionally for 10 minutes or until thickened. Season and cool.

tip Vincotto translates from Italian as 'cooked wine'; it is made by boiling down grape must (the juice and pulp of wine-making grapes) to make a thick syrup. It is available from delis and greengrocers.

goes well with grilled lamb or beef, or cheese dishes.

RUSSIAN SAUCE

prep time 10 minutes **makes** ½ cup

Combine ¼ cup whole-egg mayonnaise, 1 finely chopped shallot, 1 tablespoon tomato sauce (ketchup), 1 tablespoon finely chopped dill pickle and ½ teaspoon Tabasco sauce in a small bowl. Season to taste.

goes well with steak, grilled fish and corned beef sandwiches.

ROMESCO

prep time 10 minutes **makes** 1½ cups

Process 260g (8½-oz) jar drained roasted red capsicums (bell peppers), 1 halved clove garlic, ½ cup roasted blanched almonds, 2 tablespoons sherry vinegar, 1 teaspoon smoked paprika, 2 tablespoons chopped fresh flat-leaf parsley and ⅓ cup extra virgin olive oil until smooth. Season to taste.

goes well with grilled white fish, lamb and chicken, as well as roasted or grilled vegetables.

GREEN HUMMUS

prep time 10 minutes **makes** 2 cups

Cook 500g (1lb) frozen broad beans (fava beans) in a saucepan of boiling water for 2 minutes or until just tender; drain. Rinse under cold water; drain. Peel broad beans. Process beans with 1 clove chopped garlic, 1 cup loosely packed fresh flat-leaf parsley leaves, 2 tablespoons each fresh tarragon leaves and chopped chives, ¼ cup lemon juice, 2 tablespoons hulled tahini, ¼ cup extra virgin olive oil and 2 tablespoons water until smooth. Season to taste.

goes well with grilled fish skewers and ocean trout or salmon.

CARAMELISED RED ONIONS

prep + cook time 40 minutes **makes** 2 cups

Heat 30g (1oz) butter and 1 tablespoon olive oil in a large heavy-based frying pan over medium heat. Cook 4 medium (800g) thinly sliced red onions and 1 teaspoon sea salt, stirring frequently, for 30 minutes or until very soft and golden. Add ¼ cup red wine vinegar, 2 tablespoons maple syrup, 1 tablespoon dijon mustard and 2 teaspoons fresh thyme leaves; cook a further 5 minutes or until caramelised.

goes well with steak, pork chops and cheese sandwiches.

GRILLED KANGAROO & TREVISO WITH AGRODOLCE CHERRIES

PREP + COOK TIME 55 MINUTES (+ STANDING) **SERVES** 4

800G (1½ POUNDS) KANGAROO FILLETS

⅓ CUP (80ML) EXTRA VIRGIN OLIVE OIL

2 TEASPOONS SEA SALT FLAKES

1 TEASPOON FRESHLY GROUND BLACK PEPPER

1 SMALL RED ONION (100G), SLICED THINLY

1 SMALL CAPSICUM (BELL PEPPER) (150G), SLICED THINLY

250G (8 OUNCES) FROZEN PITTED CHERRIES

¼ CUP (60ML) RED WINE

¼ CUP (60ML) RED WINE VINEGAR

1 TABLESPOON HONEY

2 MEDIUM TREVISO (400G), HALVED LENGTHWAYS

200G (6½ OUNCES) FRESH CHERRIES, TORN

1 CUP (130G) RED-VEIN SORREL (SEE TIPS)

1 Place kangaroo in a large bowl with 1½ tablespoons of the oil, salt and pepper. Stand at room temperature for 30 minutes.

2 Meanwhile, preheat oven to 200°C/400°F.

3 Heat another 1½ tablespoons oil in a large frying pan over medium heat. Cook onion and capsicum, stirring, for 8 minutes or until softened. Add cherries, red wine, vinegar and honey; bring to a simmer over medium heat. Cook, covered, for 10 minutes. Increase heat to high; boil, crushing cherries, for 2 minutes or until thick and syrupy.

4 Preheat a barbecue (or grill plate) over high heat. Cook kangaroo for 2 minutes each side or until grill marks appear. Transfer to an oven tray; roast for 8 minutes. Transfer to a plate; rest, loosely covered, for 10 minutes.

5 Combine remaining oil and treviso in a medium bowl; season. Cook treviso on barbecue for 30 seconds each side or until grill marks appear. Transfer to a plate; cover to keep warm.

6 Cut kangaroo across the grain on the diagonal into thick slices. Arrange on a platter with treviso. Spoon over sauce; top with fresh cherries and red-vein sorrel.

nutritional count per serving 28g total fat (4g saturated fat); 2237kJ (535 cal); 20g carbohydrate; 45g protein; 5g fibre

tips You can use lamb backstraps (eye of loin) instead of the kangaroo. If treviso is unavailable, you can substitute radicchio, red witlof or red cabbage. If fresh cherries are not in season, you can use thawed frozen cherries or other red stone fruit, such as plums. You can substitute red-vein sorrel for any other purple or red leaf or herb.

GRILLED SCALLOPS & PINK GRAPEFRUIT SALAD

PREP + COOK TIME 30 MINUTES **SERVES** 4

2 MEDIUM PINK GRAPEFRUIT (850G)

2 CUPS (80G) FIRMLY PACKED TRIMMED
WATERCRESS

2 X 400G (12½-OUNCE) CANS BUTTER BEANS,
DRAINED, RINSED

3 YELLOW HEIRLOOM TOMATOES (375G),
CUT INTO WEDGES

20 SCALLOPS WITH ROE (800G), CLEANED

2 TABLESPOONS EXTRA VIRGIN OLIVE OIL

LEMON THYME & PINK GRAPEFRUIT DRESSING

2 ASIAN SHALLOTS (50G), CHOPPED FINELY

1 TEASPOON FRESH LEMON THYME LEAVES

1 TABLESPOON FINELY CHOPPED
FRESH FLAT-LEAF PARSLEY

2 TABLESPOONS EXTRA VIRGIN OLIVE OIL

1 Segment the grapefruit by peeling rind thickly so no white pith remains. Cut between membranes, over a bowl to catch the juice, releasing segments; reserve 2 tablespoons of juice for salsa. Combine watercress, beans, tomato and grapefruit segments on a large platter.

2 Make lemon thyme and pink grapefruit dressing.

3 Preheat barbecue (or grill plate) over high heat.

4 Coat scallops with the oil; season. Grill scallops for 30 seconds each side or until almost cooked through.

5 Top watercress mixture with scallops; drizzle with dressing.

lemon thyme & pink grapefruit dressing Combine ingredients with reserved grapefruit juice in a small bowl; season to taste.

nutritional count per serving 23g total fat (4g saturated fat); 2030kJ (485 cal); 30g carbohydrate; 36g protein; 8g fibre

tip You can use blood oranges or navel oranges instead of grapefruit, if you prefer.

do-ahead The salsa can be made a day ahead; store covered in the refrigerator.

GRILLED OCEAN TROUT WITH HERBED LENTILS

PREP + COOK TIME 45 MINUTES (+ STANDING) **SERVES** 4

4 X 150G (4½-OUNCE) BONELESS OCEAN TROUT FILLETS

¼ CUP (60ML) EXTRA VIRGIN OLIVE OIL

1 MEDIUM LEMON (140G)

1 MEDIUM ONION (150G), CHOPPED FINELY

2 CLOVES GARLIC, CRUSHED

3 TEASPOONS GROUND CUMIN

3 TEASPOONS GROUND CORIANDER

⅔ CUP (160G) FRENCH-STYLE GREEN LENTILS, RINSED

1½ CUPS (375ML) VEGETABLE STOCK

200G (6 OUNCES) BABY SPINACH, CHOPPED

½ CUP LOOSELY PACKED FRESH DILL SPRIGS

TANGY YOGHURT SAUCE

1 CUP (280G) GREEK-STYLE YOGHURT

¼ CUP LOOSELY PACKED FRESH DILL, CHOPPED FINELY

1 TABLESPOON DRAINED CAPERS, CHOPPED

1 Rub trout with 1 tablespoon of the oil. Finely grate lemon rind over trout; season. Juice lemon; reserve 1 tablespoon of juice for yoghurt sauce, reserve remaining juice. Cook trout, skin-side down, on a heated grill plate (or barbecue) over medium-high heat for 4 minutes each side or until done as desired; trout is best cooked to medium. Remove from heat; rest, covered, for 5 minutes.

2 Heat remaining oil in a medium frying pan over medium heat. Cook onion, garlic and spices, stirring, for 3 minutes or until lightly golden. Add lentils and stock; bring to a simmer. Simmer, covered, for 15 minutes. Remove from heat; stir in remaining lemon juice. Season to taste.

3 Make tangy yoghurt sauce.

4 Divide lentil mixture among plates; top with spinach, dill and trout. Serve with tangy yoghurt sauce.

tangy yoghurt sauce Mix yoghurt, dill, capers and reserved lemon juice in a small bowl; season to taste.

nutritional count per serving 41g total fat (9g saturated fat); 2823kJ (675 cal); 25g carbohydrate; 47g protein; 8g fibre

tip Use salmon fillets instead of ocean trout and rocket instead of spinach, if you like.

CAJUN ROAST CHICKEN WITH SPICED CHICKPEAS

PREP + COOK TIME 1 HOUR 10 MINUTES (+ STANDING) **SERVES** 4

1 TABLESPOON GROUND CINNAMON

2 TEASPOONS FRESHLY GROUND BLACK PEPPER

2 TEASPOONS SMOKED PAPRIKA

1 TEASPOON DRIED THYME

1 TEASPOON GROUND ALLSPICE

1 TEASPOON CAYENNE PEPPER

¼ TEASPOON GROUND NUTMEG

1.8KG FREE-RANGE CHICKEN, QUARTERED (SEE TIP)

1 TABLESPOON EXTRA VIRGIN OLIVE OIL

1 BUNCH FRESH CORIANDER (CILANTRO)

1 MEDIUM RED ONION (170G), SLICED THINLY

2 CLOVES GARLIC, CHOPPED FINELY

3 SLICES MIDDLE BACON (200G), CHOPPED FINELY

2 FRESH LONG GREEN CHILLIES, SEEDED, CHOPPED FINELY

2 X 400G (12½-OUNCE) CANS CHICKPEAS (GARBANZO BEANS), DRAINED, RINSED

1½ CUPS (375ML) CHICKEN STOCK

400G (12½ OUNCES) CANNED DICED TOMATOES

2 MEDIUM LIMES (180G), SLICED

1 Preheat oven to 200°C/400°F. Combine spices in a small bowl. Rub chicken all over with spice mixture; season with salt. Leave to stand at room temperature for 20 minutes.

2 Meanwhile, heat oil in a large flameproof roasting pan over medium heat. Reserve leaves from coriander; finely chop stems. Add stems to pan with onion, garlic, bacon and chilli; cook, stirring, for 5 minutes or until softened. Add chickpeas, stock and tomatoes; bring to the boil.

3 Place chicken, skin-side up, on top of chickpea mixture in pan.

4 Roast chicken, basting halfway through, for 40 minutes or until chicken is cooked through.

5 Serve chicken and spiced chickpeas with reserved coriander leaves and lime slices.

nutritional count per serving 54g total fat (16g saturated fat); 3679kJ (879 cal); 26g carbohydrate; 64g protein; 12g fibre

tip To prepare chicken, place breast-side down on a board. Using sharp kitchen scissors or poultry scissors, cut down either side of the backbone; discard. Cut chicken in half along centre of breastbone; cut in half crossways to yield four joints. Tuck wing tips under.

TURKEY PARMIGIANA WITH SHAKE & BAKE WEDGES

PREP + COOK TIME 1 HOUR 15 MINUTES **SERVES** 4

500G (1 POUND) TURKEY BREASTS, CUT
HORIZONTALLY INTO 4 THICK SLICES

2 EGGS

1 CUP (120G) ALMOND MEAL

1 CLOVE GARLIC, CRUSHED

¼ CUP (60ML) OLIVE OIL

⅔ CUP (175G) PASTA SAUCE

120G (4 OUNCES) BOCCONCINI, SLICED THINLY

2 GEM LETTUCE (360G), CUT INTO WEDGES

SHAKE & BAKE WEDGES

1 TABLESPOON OLIVE OIL

1 SMALL ORANGE SWEET POTATO (250G),
CUT INTO WEDGES

1 LARGE PARSNIP (350G), CUT INTO WEDGES

1 TEASPOON MEXICAN SPICE MIX

1 BUNCH BABY BEETROOT (500G),
CUT INTO WEDGES

1 Preheat oven to 220°C/425°F.

2 Make shake and bake wedges.

3 Meanwhile, pound turkey between two sheets of plastic wrap or baking paper until 5mm (¼-inch) thick.

4 Lightly beat eggs in a shallow dish. Combine almond meal and garlic in another shallow dish; season. Dip turkey, one piece at a time, in egg, then in almond mixture to coat, pressing firmly.

5 Heat half the oil in a large frying pan over medium-high heat. Cook two turkey slices for 2 minutes each side or until browned. Drain on paper towel; wipe pan clean. Repeat with remaining oil and turkey.

6 Transfer turkey to an oven tray lined with baking paper. Spoon pasta sauce evenly over turkey; top with bocconcini. Bake turkey for 5 minutes or until cheese is melted and turkey is just cooked through.

7 Serve turkey parmigiana with wedges and lettuce.

shake & bake wedges Line a large oven tray with baking paper; brush paper with the oil. Place the sweet potato and parsnip wedges, ⅔ of the spice mix and a little sea salt in a large snap lock bag or freezer bag; shake to combine. Spread wedges over tray. Repeat with beetroot (this stops the beetroot staining the other vegetables). Bake wedges for 40 minutes, turning once, or until golden and tender.

nutritional count per serving 51g total fat (10g saturated fat); 3289kJ (786 cal); 29g carbohydrate; 48g protein; 13g fibre

tips We used a napolitana pasta sauce. You can use chicken instead of turkey, if you like.

do-ahead The turkey can be crumbed up to 4 hours ahead; keep covered in the fridge.

GLOSSARY

AGAVE SYRUP from the agave plant; has a low GI, but that is due to the high percentage of fructose present, which may be harmful in large quantities.

BEANS

black also called turtle beans or black kidney beans; an earthy-flavoured dried bean completely different from the better-known Chinese black beans (fermented soybeans).

broad (fava) available dried, fresh, canned and frozen. Fresh should be peeled twice (discarding the outer long green pod and the beige-green tough inner shell); frozen beans have had their pods removed but the beige shell still needs removal.

butter cans labelled butter beans are, in fact, cannellini beans. Confusingly butter is also another name for lima beans (dried and canned); a large beige bean having a mealy texture and mild taste.

cannellini a small white bean similar in appearance and flavour to other white beans (great northern, navy or haricot), all of which can be substituted for the other. Available dried or canned.

green also known as french or string beans (although the tough string they once had has generally been bred out of them), this long thin fresh bean is consumed in its entirety once cooked.

sprouts tender new growths of assorted beans and seeds germinated for consumption as sprouts.

BREADCRUMBS, PANKO (JAPANESE) are available in two varieties: larger pieces and fine crumbs. Both have a lighter texture than Western-style breadcrumbs. They are available from Asian grocery stores and most supermarkets.

BUTTERMILK originally the term given to the slightly sour liquid left after butter was churned from cream, today it is made from no-fat or low-fat milk to which specific bacterial cultures have been added. Despite its name, it is actually low in fat.

CAPERS grey-green buds of a warm climate shrub (usually Mediterranean); sold dried and salted or pickled in a vinegar brine. Rinse before using.

CAVOLO NERO also known as tuscan cabbage. Has long, narrow, wrinkled leaves and a rich and astringent, mild cabbage flavour. It doesn't lose its volume like silver beet or spinach when cooked, but it does need longer cooking.

CELERIAC (CELERY ROOT) tuberous root with knobbly brown skin, white flesh and a celery-like flavour. Keep peeled celeriac in acidulated water to stop it discolouring.

CHEESE

cheddar the most common cow-milk 'tasty' cheese; should be aged, hard and have a pronounced bite.

cottage fresh, white, unripened curd cheese with a grainy consistency and a fat content of 15% to 55%.

cream commonly called philadelphia or philly; a soft cow-milk cheese, its fat content ranges from 14 to 33%.

fetta Greek in origin; a crumbly textured goat- or sheep-milk cheese having a sharp, salty taste. Ripened and stored in salted whey.

goat's made from goat's milk, has an earthy, strong taste; available in both soft and firm textures, in various shapes and sizes, and sometimes rolled in ash or herbs.

gorgonzola a creamy Italian blue cheese with a mild, sweet taste; good as an accompaniment to fruit or used to flavour sauces.

gruyère a hard-rind Swiss cheese with small holes and a nutty, slightly salty flavour.

haloumi a firm, cream-coloured sheep-milk cheese matured in brine; haloumi can be grilled or fried without breaking down. Should be eaten while still warm as it becomes rubbery on cooling.

mozzarella soft, spun-curd cheese; originating in southern Italy where it was traditionally made from water-buffalo milk. Now generally made from cow's milk, it is the most popular pizza cheese because of its low melting point and elasticity when heated.

parmesan also called parmigiano; is a hard, grainy cow-milk cheese originating in Italy. Reggiano is the best variety.

pecorino the Italian generic name for cheeses made from sheep-milk; hard, white to pale-yellow in colour. If you can't find it, use parmesan instead.

ricotta a soft, sweet, moist, white cow-milk cheese with a low fat content and a slightly grainy texture. The name roughly translates as 'cooked again' and refers to ricotta's manufacture from a whey that is itself a by-product of other cheese making.

CHILLI

cayenne pepper a long, thin-fleshed, extremely hot red chilli usually sold dried and ground.

flakes also sold as crushed chilli; dehydrated deep-red extremely fine slices and whole seeds.

green any unripened chilli; also some particular varieties that are ripe when green, such as jalapeño, habanero, poblano or serrano.

jalapeño pronounced hah-lah-pain-yo. Fairly hot, medium-sized, plump, dark green chilli; available pickled, sold canned or bottled, and fresh, from greengrocers.

long available both fresh and dried; a generic term used for any moderately hot, thin, long (6-8cm/2¼-3¼ inch) chilli.

powder can be used as a substitute for fresh chillies (½ teaspoon ground chilli powder to 1 chopped medium fresh chilli).

CRÈME FRAÎCHE a mature, naturally fermented cream (minimum fat content 35%) having a velvety texture and slightly tangy, nutty flavour.

DAIKON also called white radish; this long, white horseradish has a wonderful, sweet flavour. The flesh is white but the skin can be either white or black; buy those that are firm and unwrinkled.

EDAMAME (SOY BEANS) available frozen from Asian food stores and some supermarkets.

FISH SAUCE called nam pla (Thai) or nuoc nam (Vietnamese); made from pulverised salted fermented fish, most often anchovies. Has a pungent smell and strong taste, so use sparingly.

FIVE-SPICE POWDER (CHINESE FIVE-SPICE) a fragrant mixture of ground cinnamon, cloves, star anise, sichuan pepper and fennel seeds.

FLOUR

chickpea (besan) creamy yellow flour made from chickpeas; it is very nutritious.

plain (all-purpose) a general all-purpose wheat flour.

wholemeal also known as wholewheat flour; milled with the wheat germ so is higher in fibre and more nutritional than plain flour.

FREEKEH is cracked roasted green wheat and can be found in some larger supermarkets, health food and specialty food stores.

GAI LAN also known as chinese broccoli, gai larn, kanah, gai lum and chinese kale; used more for its stems than its coarse leaves.

GHEE a type of clarified butter used in Indian cooking; milk solids are cooked until golden brown, which imparts a nutty flavour and sweet aroma; it can be heated to a high temperature without burning.

HARISSA a Moroccan paste made from dried chillies, cumin, garlic, oil and caraway seeds. Available from Middle Eastern food shops and supermarkets.

KECAP MANIS a thick soy sauce with added sugar and spices. The sweetness comes from the addition of molasses or palm sugar.

LSA A ground mixture of linseeds (L), sunflower seeds (S) and almonds (A); available from supermarkets and health food stores.

MAPLE SYRUP, PURE distilled from the sap of sugar maple trees found only in Canada and the USA. Maple-flavoured syrup or pancake syrup is not an adequate substitute for the real thing.

MIRIN a Japanese champagne-coloured cooking wine; made of glutinous rice and alcohol and used expressly for cooking. Should not be confused with sake.

NORI a type of dried seaweed used as a flavouring, garnish or for sushi. Sold in thin sheets, plain or toasted (yaki-nori).

OIL

coconut is extracted from the coconut flesh, the best quality is virgin oil, which is the oil pressed from the dried coconut flesh, and doesn't include the use of solvents or other refining processes.

olive made from ripened olives. Extra virgin and virgin are the first and second press, respectively, of the olives; "light" refers to taste not fat levels.

peanut pressed from ground peanuts; most commonly used oil in Asian cooking because of its high smoke point (capacity to handle high heat without burning).

sesame used as a flavouring rather than a cooking medium.

vegetable oils sourced from plant rather than animal fats.

ONIONS

green (scallions) also called, incorrectly, shallot; an immature onion picked before the bulb has formed, has a long, bright-green stalk.

red also known as spanish, red spanish or bermuda onion; a sweet-flavoured, large, purple-red onion.

shallots also called french or golden shallots or eschalots; small and brown-skinned.

POLENTA also known as cornmeal; a flour-like cereal made of ground corn (maize). Also the name of the dish made from it.

QUINOA pronounced keen-wa; is the seed of a leafy plant similar to spinach. It has a delicate, slightly nutty taste and chewy texture.

flakes the grains have been rolled and flattened.

RADICCHIO a red-leafed Italian chicory with a refreshing bitter taste that's eaten raw and grilled. Comes in varieties named after their places of origin, such as round-headed Verona or long-headed Treviso.

RICE MALT SYRUP also known as brown rice syrup or rice syrup; is made by cooking brown rice flour with enzymes to break down its starch into sugars from which the water is removed.

TAHINI a rich, sesame-seed paste, used in most Middle-Eastern cuisines, especially Lebanese, in dips and sauces.

TAMARI a thick, dark soy sauce made mainly from soya beans, but without the wheat used in most standard soy sauces.

TAMARIND CONCENTRATE (OR PASTE) the distillation of tamarind pulp into a condensed, compacted paste. Thick and purple-black, it requires no soaking. Found in Asian food stores.

TOFU also called bean curd; an off-white, custard-like product made from the "milk" of crushed soybeans. Comes fresh as soft or firm, and processed as fried or pressed dried sheets. Fresh tofu can be refrigerated in water (changed daily) for up to 4 days.

TURMERIC also called kamin; is a rhizome related to galangal and ginger. Must be grated or pounded to release its acrid aroma and pungent flavour. Known for the golden colour it imparts, fresh turmeric can be substituted with the more commonly found dried powder.

WATERCRESS one of the cress family, a large group of peppery greens. Highly perishable, so must be used as soon as possible after purchase.

WOMBOK (NAPA CABBAGE) also known as peking or chinese cabbage. Elongated in shape with pale green, crinkly leaves.

XANTHAN GUM is a thickening agent produced by fermentation of, usually, corn sugar. When buying xanthan gum, ensure the packet states 'made from fermented corn sugar'. Found in the health-food section in larger supermarkets.

YOGHURT, GREEK-STYLE plain yoghurt strained in a cloth (muslin) to remove the whey and to give it a creamy consistency.

CONVERSION CHART

MEASURES

One Australian metric measuring cup holds approximately 250ml; one Australian metric tablespoon holds 20ml; one Australian metric teaspoon holds 5ml.

The difference between one country's measuring cups and another's is within a two- or three-teaspoon variance, and will not affect your cooking results. North America, New Zealand and the United Kingdom use a 15ml tablespoon.

All cup and spoon measurements are level. The most accurate way of measuring dry ingredients is to weigh them. When measuring liquids, use a clear glass or plastic jug with the metric markings.

The imperial measurements used in these recipes are approximate only. Measurements for cake pans are approximate only. Using same-shaped cake pans of a similar size should not affect your baking. We measure the inside top of the cake pan to determine sizes.

We use large eggs with an average weight of 60g.

DRY MEASURES

METRIC	IMPERIAL
15G	½OZ
30G	1OZ
60G	2OZ
90G	3OZ
125G	4OZ (¼LB)
155G	5OZ
185G	6OZ
220G	7OZ
250G	8OZ (½LB)
280G	9OZ
315G	10OZ
345G	11OZ
375G	12OZ (¾LB)
410G	13OZ
440G	14OZ
470G	15OZ
500G	16OZ (1LB)
750G	24OZ (1½LB)
1KG	32OZ (2LB)

LIQUID MEASURES

METRIC	IMPERIAL
30ML	1 FLUID OZ
60ML	2 FLUID OZ
100ML	3 FLUID OZ
125ML	4 FLUID OZ
150ML	5 FLUID OZ
190ML	6 FLUID OZ
250ML	8 FLUID OZ
300ML	10 FLUID OZ
500ML	16 FLUID OZ
600ML	20 FLUID OZ
1000ML (1 LITRE)	1¾ PINTS

LENGTH MEASURES

METRIC	IMPERIAL
3MM	⅛IN
6MM	¼IN
1CM	½IN
2CM	¾IN
2.5CM	1IN
5CM	2IN
6CM	2½IN
8CM	3IN
10CM	4IN
13CM	5IN
15CM	6IN
18CM	7IN
20CM	8IN
22CM	9IN
25CM	10IN
28CM	11IN
30CM	12IN (1FT)

OVEN TEMPERATURES

The oven temperatures in this book are for conventional ovens; if you have a fan-forced oven, decrease the temperature by 10-20 degrees.

	°C (CELSIUS)	°F (FAHRENHEIT)
VERY SLOW	120	250
SLOW	150	300
MODERATELY SLOW	160	325
MODERATE	180	350
MODERATELY HOT	200	400
HOT	220	425
VERY HOT	240	475

INDEX